THE
BIG BOOK
OF WATERCOLOR

THE
BIG BOOK
OF WATERCOLOR

**The history, the studio, the materials
the techniques, the subjects, the theory
and the practice of watercolor painting**

by

JOSÉ M. PARRAMÓN

WATSON—GUPTILL PUBLICATIONS / NEW YORK

José M.ª Parramón, *Villar del Saz (Cuenca)*. Private Collection.

Contents

To Maria, my wife

José M.ª Parramón, *A snowy landscape.* Private Collection.

3

J. M.ª Parramón. *Port of Genoa.*
Private Collection.

introduction

Painting as a hobby, only a hobby...?
It sounds fine. But there are hobbies that never take off, they never quite crystalize, because they are not taken seriously. Can you imagine someone who plays the piano for a hobby but only sits down to practice once a month?

Painting is like the piano: one must play it often. It has its technique, its mechanics, its skills. Likewise, one must paint often, even more so in watercolors.

It is a process, as you well know, which requires assiduous practice; the more one paints, the better. Van Gogh, who was an indefatigable worker—close to 850 paintings and more than 1000 drawings in the last year of his life!— was pleased to quote a remark on watercolors made by the Impressionist, Whistler: "Yes, I painted it in two hours, but I worked for years in order to be able to do it in two hours."

Painting in watercolors is most certainly an art for amateurs with the will and capacity to work:

An art which must be learned and practiced

In this book, I have tried to bring together the knowledge necessary to learn to paint in watercolors. I have researched and written, first, about the history of watercolors, so that you may know when, who, why, and how the first watercolor painters painted, and along the way I discovered, some early figures—such as the Academy of Dr. Monro, in London—which filled me with surprise. I have brought together all manner of information and pictures, by and about everybody, in order to inform you with regard to furniture, materials, and tools for watercolor painting; I comment on the different types and qualities available, and give my opinion of different brushes, colors, papers, etc. I have dedicated an important part of this book to explaining, by means of pictures and practical examples, the habits and techniques of professional artists, from the different systems for absorbing and reducing colors, to the different procedures for "opening up" white spaces before or after painting, wet or dry. I have painted wet in wet, and I have brought color theories into practical use by proposing a series of practical exercises beginning with painting with only three colors, which tests and proves that all of the colors found in Nature may be made with only the three primary colors.

I have applied to painting in watercolors, all of the laws, rules, experiences, and findings which I know after many years of teaching art, in the areas of drawing, color, mixing, colors, composition, interpretation, and blending. And finally, I have carried out a series of demonstrations—some with the cooperation of my friends, leading names in Spanish watercolor painting—in which I explain step by step and in a practical manner the lessons contained in this book.

It is a book illustrated with active and instructive illustrations—450 in all—and it is a book to take part in, with practical exercises you can carry out in color mixing, perspective, composition, and other technical lessons.

Ah, but we must play our whole hand! I have done all I can and all I know how to do. Now it is your turn. It's not enough to say that you haven't the time or that you don't feel inspired. "Waiting for inspiration is a vain act," said Balzac, "one must begin, take up the material and get one's hands dirty."

introduction

Beginning to paint, like any intellectual process, always requires effort, "we try to put it off with all type of excuses, the pencil is dull, the palette is dirty..." Yes, but it is also almost always true that, no sooner do we start than we feel an uncontainable passion to continue to work. When this passion is cultivated, it becomes a habit: the *habit of working*.

Van Gogh acquired this habit of working from the first day, with all the passion which is reflected in his paintings:

"From the time I bought my first colors and painting tools, I have been coming and going, painting all day and finishing exhausted. I haven't been able to contain myself, I haven't been able to hold myself back nor stop working."

I hope this book will help you to begin to feel a passion for painting in watercolors.

José M. Parramón.

4

Federico Lloveras. *Embarcadero*. Private Collection.

history
of watercolor
painting

origins

Man has been writing and illustrating books for 3,500 years.

It was originally on the banks of the Nile in Egypt that a fibrous plant named *cyperus papyrus* was discovered whose bark, cut into strips, could be rolled into a scroll. These rolls of papyrus were used to write and illustrate scrolls dealing with science, history, magic, and religion. Another important use was that of burying the scrolls with the dead as an aid in their journey to the other world. The writings were to help them explain their deeds to Osiris, judge of the dead. The images in these scrolls, known since then as miniatures, were painted with transparent colors. The pigments used for ochres and siennas came from the earth; red came from minerals such as cinnabar; azurite was used to obtain blue; malachite for green; cropiment for yellow, and rexalgar for orange. Black was made from burnt willow wood; chalk produced white. These pigments were blended with gum arabic and egg white and were applied diluted in water. In short, they were watercolors.

One thousand years later, around 170 BC, parchment was used for the first time by Eumenes II, king of Pergamum. This new writing surface was obtained from sheep or goat skin treated with lime and sheared and softened with a pumice stone. These parchment sheets were joined into small notebooks known as codices which were in turn joined to form a book called a codex. Parchment has been used ever since to make manuscripts.

Until the 9th century most miniatures, whether in Greece, Rome, Syria, or Byzantium, were painted from a mixture of watercolor and lead white, producing an opaque watercolor. The 9th century marked the beginning of the reign of Charlemagne, emperor of the Carolingians.

Charlemagne placed great importance on the creation of manuscripts; he found great artists who alternated in the use of both opaque and transparent watercolors. This mixture was used during the late Middle Ages and even reached the Renaissance when the use of watercolors in miniature paintings became common.

These are in effect, the origins of watercolor painting.

Fig. 6—*Opening of the Mouth*, Hunefer mummy from the book of the dead of the same person, papyrus from the 13th century B.C., British Museum, London.

Fig. 7—(Below) *Adam and Eve*, page from a Bible manuscript by Alcuin or Moutier Grandval, from the Carolingian period. 834-43 A.D., watercolor on parchment, British Museum, London.

Fig. 8—(Above) Francesco Pesellino, *Allegory of Rome*, miniature, gouache on parchment; borders of the frame painted in watercolor. From the manuscript *De Secundo Bello Punico Poema*, 1447-55, Hermitage Museum, Leningrad.

Fig. 9—(Right) Page from the manuscript on the *Poems* of Charles d'Orléans (imprisoned in the Tower of London around 1500), watercolor and gouache on parchment, British Museum, London.

dürer: the first "watercolorist"

Albrecht Dürer from Nuremberg, who was described as "ardent and austere" by the painter Cornelius, was the greatest German painter and engraver of the 16th century. During his lifetime (1471-1528) he wrote three books, executed over 1000 drawings, almost 250 woodcuts, 100 copper engravings, and painted a grand total of 188 canvases, of which 86 were watercolors. Dürer's first known painting is a watercolor landscape which he painted at the age of eighteen. All this is quite amazing. Very few people know that Dürer alternated between oil and watercolor painting. Although his oil paintings, such as *Adam and Eve* and *Self-Portrait with Gloves*, both in the Prado in Madrid, are well known, few people are aware that he did watercolor paintings as good as the landscape shown here. Why is it that watercolors are not considered on a level with oil paintings? As we will learn later on, the use of watercolor for its own sake did not gain recognition until the latter part of the 18th century. During Dürer's time watercolors were said to

Fig. 10—Albrecht Dürer, *Wing of a Small Blue Bird,* watercolor on parchment, Albertina, Vienna.

Fig. 11—Albrecht Dürer, *View of Kalchreuth*, watercolor on paper, previously in Bremen, Kunsthalle.

10

11

dürer: the first "watercolorist"

12

Fig. 12—Albrecht Dürer, *Self-Portrait with Gloves,* (detail), The Prado, Madrid. In this painting there is an inscription in German that reads: "I have painted this portrait according to my features at the age of twenty-six." This self-portrait in oils was painted the same year (1498) that Dürer did the series of engravings of the Apocalypse that brought him international fame. Dürer is said to have wanted to emphasize his mastery and merit as an artist and man of letters in this self-portrait.

Fig. 13—Albrecht Dürer, *The Large Piece of Turf,* watercolor on paper, Albertina, Vienna. In contrast with the landscape on the previous page—loose, carefree, with a style and brushstroke comparable to those of a modern artist—Dürer offers us here a detailed, hyper-realist finish, in which opaque watercolor is used with sureness. The work, 41 cm × 31.5 cm (16" × 12.5"), was painted from nature, as was customary with Dürer who, according to his biographers, felt a true passion for animals and nature.

13

serve a documentary function. They were the first draft of a future oil painting. This underestimation of watercolor was still evident in the early part of the 20th century. During the 1930s the Tietze brothers, who wrote the most complete catalog of Dürer's work, did not add a separate chapter for his watercolors, but instead meshed them with the sketches. Other authors who have written about Dürer, such as Lippman, Winkler, and Panofsky, have followed their classification.

Albrecht Dürer was undoubtedly one of the

14

forerunners of watercolor. His example, however, was not followed by artists after him. For close to 300 years watercolor remained a step in the process of oil painting.

Fig. 14—Albrecht Dürer, *The Hare,* watercolor on paper, Albertina, Vienna. In the course of his life as an artist, Dürer painted various animals: horses, lions, a crab, a parrot, squirrels, a lobster, and even a sea lion, always with the preciousness of this hare, always in watercolor, although, as with this model, he sometimes used opaque watercolors to outline, for example, light fur on a dark background. Dürer always painted from nature; critics and students assure us that this hare was caught alive and shut in a room where the artist painted it. To prove this assertion they say that a window is reflected in the animal's eye and that its shadow falls on a smooth floor. If so, Dürer painted from nature, with the model in front of him, but he also painted from memory, using the model as a live reference that he consulted as it moved.

watercolor as an aid: 16th and 17th centuries

Dürer was an exception. Fifty years before him, Jacobo Bellini had painted some watercolors as preliminary sketches, which served as inspiration for the paintings and murals of his sons, Gentile and Giovanni, and his son-in-law Mantegna. Bellini, however, never really painted with watercolor.

Watercolor for its own sake disappeared after Dürer. However, it was frequently used as an aid for oil painting. This technique is most common among the Flemish artists, specifically Rubens.

Peter Paul Rubens painted close to 1000 paintings (to be exact, Bodart's catalog names 993). A great part of his work consisted of large paintings used to decorate churches and palaces. His famous cycle of 24 paintings on the life of Marie de Medici, now in the Louvre, is made up of panels that measure 3.94 × 2.95m. Its central work, *Henry IV*, measures 3.94 × 7.27m. Rubens organized his workshop in a way that facilitated the creation of many paintings of large proportions. His young assitants, such as van Dyck, Jordaens, and Snyders, later achieved independent recognition. Rubens would first draw a preliminary sketch and then paint a watercolor. From this watercolor draft he painted a scaled-down preliminary work. Then his assistants were given all the sketches and they painted the original almost to completion, leaving Rubens the job of applying the final touches.

When Anthony van Dyck left Rubens's workshop, he traveled to England. He painted some watercolor landscapes which he would later use as backdrops to his oil portraits. Jacob Jordaens used watercolors as a young man in cartoons for tapestries. He stayed with Rubens until the latter's death. Jordaens tried to follow in his master's footsteps by continuing Rubens's technique of using small watercolor sketches.

This use of watercolor is seen throughout Europe during the 16th and 17th centuries. The only exception is Holland where van Avercamp, van Everdingen and the van Ostade brothers, among others, painted watercolor sketches and first drafts which they would sell to craftsmen and to the petit bourgeoisie of Amsterdam.

Figs. 15, 16, 17—(Above) Rubens, *The Stoning of St. Stephen*, watercolor sketch, Hermitage Museum, Leningrad. (Right, fig. 16.) Sketch in oil, Royal Palace, Brussels. (Right, fig. 17.) Final rendering of *The Stoning of St. Stephen*, Museum of Fine Arts, Valenciennes.

16

Fig. 18—Anthony van Dyck, *Landscape at Birmingham Port,* Barbierov Institute of Fine Arts, Moscow. It is believed that during his second stay in England, from 1632 until his death in 1641, van Dyck painted several landscapes in watercolor that served as studies and models for oil painting and as backgrounds for some of his portraits.

18

20

Fig. 19—Adriaen van Ostade, *Peasants,* Hermitage Museum, Leningrad. In the 17th century, when watercolor painting was an aid to oil painting, some Dutch artists painted small watercolors on popular themes, which were sold to craftsmen and the petit bourgeoisie of Amsterdam.

Fig. 20—Jacob Jordaens, *The Arribal,* British Museum, London. When Rubens died, Jordaens tried to continue his master's work and he even finished the uncompleted paintings that Spain had commissioned Rubens to do. He later followed Rubens's work methods very closely, studying watercolor sketches prior to completing his works in oil.

19

monochromatic watercolor

According to Cennino Cennini, an Italian artist and educator, during the Renaissance and after, in the 16th and 17th centuries, all artists used watercolor... with only one color. In his book *Libro dell'Arte* (1390) he says: "After accentuating the design you will give shading to the shapes by using ink washes. It is necessary to use the amount of water that fits in a nutshell with two ink drops. The shading must be done with a brush made of hair from a sable's tail. When the washes must be darker the same technique should be applied but more ink drops should be used."

Cennini's book merely explains artistic procedures that were already in use during the 14th century. Thus, from Giotto to the mid-18th century, 400 years later, when watercolor paint began to be used for finished works, artists in general painted according to Cennini's formula.

For example: Raphael's frescoes in the Stanza della Signatura. Raphael was commissioned by Pope Julius II between 1509 and 1511 to paint some murals for the Pope's new rooms in the Vatican palace. Different museums now house the preliminary sketches and studies of figures and parts of the body in foreshortened perspectives, as well as the final cartoon, a monochrome watercolor painted with two sepia colors. (fig. 20, mural project *The School of Athens* from the Stanza della Signatura). This work method was followed by Raphael, Leonardo, and Michelangelo whenever they had to paint an important mural or painting.

Monochromatic watercolor was also the medium used when sketching outdoors. On these occasions the paper used was gray or was painted previously with a yellow or ochre background. This was then painted with sepia and water according to Cennini's formula. These sketches were only used as notes and as an aid when doing an oil painting.

21

22

Fig. 21—Raphael, *The School of Athens*, project painted in watercolor. Ambrosiana, Milan.

Fig. 22—Raphael, *The School of Athens*, fresco in the Stanza della Segnatura, Vatican, Rome. Observe the differences between the final painting and the project painted in wash in shades of sepia. Several figures were added for the final picture, but the projection shows the exact character of the figures, their form, expression, position, light and shadow, etc., enabling Raphael's assistants to work more easily when doing the actual fresco.

Fig. 23—Salvator Rosa, *Study of Trees*, wash, Hermitage Museum, Leningrad. The dexterity, sureness, and skill with which this study of trees was done is of a quality comparable to the resolution of a professional watercolor artist of today.

Fig. 24—Guercino, *Landscape with a Volcano*, British Museum, London. This is an example of the use of sepia wash on gray paper. In this wash we can see the artist's skill and knowledge of the medium in the way in which he indicates the model's position and the effects of light and shadow. He even adds a few figures to help the viewer understand distances and proportions, all with just a few brushstrokes.

wash: forerunner of watercolor

In the historical evolution of watercolor we must also mention Rembrandt. For although Rembrandt never painted watercolors, he made hundreds of sketches in brown bistre or sepia wash (this last made from the "ink" of the cuttlefish) with such skill and practice he was able to successfully reflect volume, shadow, darkness and... such color: These sketches were Rembrandt's color notes.

While Rembrandt worked in Amsterdam, Claude Lorraine was busy painting landscapes in Rome. His landscapes were of enormous proportions and were commissioned by clergymen and kings such as Urban VIII and Philip IV of Spain. Constable, the well-known British landscape artist, said the following in one communication to the Royal Academy of London: "It has been said that Lorraine is the best landscape artist in the world and this is well-deserved praise. His main attribute is the mixture of splendor with quietude, color with freshness, shadow and light." Lorraine would first make a preliminary wash sketch of his idea and would then go to the countryside and would continue the process out of doors. He used two or three colors in the same range: sienna, sepia, umber. His landscapes in oils, which often measured up to 2.5 × 2 m, would require at least eight wash drawings as well as some pencil or charcoal sketches before completion. It tok him two months to complete a painting.

The same can be said of Frenchman Nicolas Poussin who, together with Claude Lorraine, is considered an innovator of the English landscape school. These two artists were undoubtedly a great influence on the group of English artists who used watercolor from the 18th century on. Nicolas Poussin alternated religious or mythological figure paintings with landscapes in which mythological figures also appeared. Poussin worked, as did Lorraine, from a series of preliminary wash sketches drawn from nature. In some of his sketches made with just two colors and occasionally black, the richness of tones and range of light are so marvelous that they seem to be actual color notes.

Like many 17th century artists, Rembrandt, Lorraine, and Poussin did not yet use watercolor. However, they gave wash, which was a procedure which required techniques similar to those of watercolor, its own place as something more than just an aid in oil painting. At this point all that was needed was one factor that would give watercolor the necessary push. This happened with the "Grand Tour."

25

Fig. 25—Rembrandt, *Figure Study*, Rijksmuseum, Amsterdam. As this sketch shows, Rembrandt's mastery of wash was incredible. This mastery derives from an absolute sureness in constructing and drawing.

26

27

Fig. 26—Claude Lorraine, *Landscape with River, View of the Tiber from Monte Mario, Rome,* British Museum, London.

Fig. 27—Nicolas Poussin, *The Moller Bridge Near Rome,* Albertina Museum, Vienna.

the 18th century: the english discover rome

The English "discovered" Rome toward the middle of the 18th century. At this time King George II was adamantly trying to transform England from an agricultural country into an industrial and commercial nation. Small cottage industries were being replaced by factories, and commerce was looking to broaden its horizons overseas and in the colonies. Hundreds of businessmen, industrialists, intellectuals, artists, and aristocrats traveled frequently between England and the Continent. Traveling was fashionable. It was the century of the "Grand Tour."

The popular itinerary was France, Switzerland and Italy, with Rome as the final destination. Once there, it was a must to visit the Colosseum, the Arch of Titus, the public baths of Caracalla. Ruins were also in fashion. It was the century of the Grand Tour and the period of Neoclassical Art.

Touring and the "discovery" of Rome had a great influence on English taste in art. The first stop in Paris led the English tourists to the Louvre where they could admire the great paintings of Poussin and Lorraine. These two pioneers of the Neoclassical style painted classical figures and ruins into their wonderful romantic landscapes. During their stay in Switzerland, the English were able to cross the Alps and live in close contact with "Nature," the subject of an almost religious cult at the time. Finally, they would reach Italy and admire the classic beauty of ancient Rome. Every experience and sensation made the tourists want to return to London with a pictorial souvenir of their trip to the "Eternal City."

These pictorial souvenirs were etchings printed in black or sepia. They could already be bought in Rome and Venice in the early 18th century. By 1703 Lucas Carlevari had already published 103 of his engraved views of Venice. Giovanni Antonio Canaletto, famous for his *vedutas* (views) of Venice and Rome, signed a contract in 1730 with Joseph Smith, later the British consul, for the sale and distribution of over 140 etchings in Britain. In 1745 Piranesi published 135 *vedutas* of ancient Rome. Thousands of copies of these were printed.

The production of *vedutas* was constantly being expanded upon by the many European artists who began to do this type of work. These include the Italians Ricci, Panini, and Guardi, and the English Pars, Grimm, Rooker, and Cozens, among others. By this time, also, the English were printing a large number of illustrations from copper etchings or engravings in

28

black and sepia which portrayed landscapes, cityscapes, monuments, flowers, still lifes, horses, and dogs, among other things. These drawings, made by artists called "topographers," served as decoration for the walls of private homes. It occurred to someone, inspired by Italian *vedutas*, that the etchings would be enhanced if they were colored with transparent watercolors. Shortly thereafter the color became more and more important until finally the drawings appeared to be painted rather than etched.

Paul Sandby, known as the "father of English watercolor," was one of the artists involved in the transformation of drawings into paintings. Although Paul Sandby did not travel to Italy, he followed the "Grand Tour" phenomenon closely. He sketched and etched many ruins which he would then illuminate with watercolor. His desire to make each watercolor a unique work of art rather than a means to an end allowed him to study and experiment with different formulas.

Paul Sandby and his brother Thomas — also a watercolor painter and topographical draughtsman for the government — were founding members of the Royal Academy of London. Paul also painted pictures in watercolor and gouache of urban and rural landscapes. Outstanding among the latter were his renderings, often directly from nature, of the Great Royal Wood, Windsor Park, of Windsor Castle where Thomas was keeper. Sandby was twenty-seven in 1752 when he started painting these forests. His technique and style was to greatly influence other English watercolor landscape paint-

Fig. 28—John Robert Cozens, *Cetara, a Fishermen's Village in the Gulf of Salerno.* Mrs. Cecil Keith Collection, England. It was J. R. Cozens who broke with the English tradition of "illuminated drawings" and began to paint and delineate forms with color and tone, instead of line.

29

Fig. 29—Francis Cotes, *Portrait of Paul Sandby,* Tate Gallery, London.

30

ers including William Pars, Francis Towne, Thomas Rowlandson, Francis Wheatley, and the especially noteworthy John Robert Cozens. William Pars traveled to Greece when he was twenty-two as the artist for an archeological dig. He became well known for his drawings of the dig. Some years later he went to Rome, where he lived until his death in 1872. His companions in Rome included Cozens, Jones, and his close friend Towne. William Pars quickly embraced the idea of painting without the sharp outlines made with a pen or pencil. His watercolors of old buildings are truly wonderful works of art.

Francis Towne, on the other hand, used sharp contours and more daring colors to illuminate his figures. Rowlandson was a well known caricaturist, and his personality was apparent in his portraits and landscapes. Wheatley introduced a palette of bright colors with reds, blues, and yellows in his rural landscapes with figures.

John Robert Cozens learned his trade from his father. He was described by Constable as "a brilliant landscape artist, all poetry." Cozens used a limited palette of greens, blues, siennas, and grays but the composition of each painting was studied to such a degree that each of his pictures was really like a poem. He profoundly influenced the Romantic Period in England and the artists of the next generation such as Girtin and Turner.

the english national art

In the spring of 1804 the first society of water-color artists, the Old Water-Colour Society, was founded. One year later, also for the first time in the world, an exposition of watercolor paintings was held.

In England, of course.

Until then, the members of the Royal Academy of London, which was already thirty years old, had very discriminatory policies toward watercolor artists. Watercolors were only allowed into a show if the artist also had oil paintings. Furthermore, the watercolors were always off to the side, with the most visible and best-lit areas of the salon being reserved for oil paintings. This lack of importance given to their work angered the artists into founding a separate society and organizing their own showing at a different salon — which succeeded in attracting the public and buying customers.

By the late 18th century the merit and value of watercolor as a medium in itself was recognized, and was used as means of expression by such renowned artists as Hogarth, Reynolds, and Gainsborough.

Artists were no longer limited to landscapes; they now went indoors to paint figures and still life scenes. In this new area both William Blake and John Henry Fuseli showed extraordinary talent and imaginative power. Fuseli's paintings are characterized by the exaggerated drawing of the movements and gestures of the figures. William Blake wrote poems which he would then illustrate with watercolors and publish. Among his best-known works are the watercolors illustrating the Book of Job, Dante's poems, and his critique of the Age of Reason.

By this time, thousands of amateurs were painting watercolors in England. It was already the "English National Art," as it was to be named years later by the journalist Edmond About in his reports on the International Exhibition in Paris.

31

32

Fig. 31—William Blake, *The Simoniac Pope*, Tate Gallery, London. Blake was an inspired and ingenious artist, poet, painter, and engraver, who once wrote and illustrated his own poems on the Bible, Milton, Shakespeare, and Dante, interpreting the texts of these works and authors and demonstrating extraordinary ability and imagination.

Fig. 32—John Henry Fuseli, *Kriemhild in a Dream Sees Siegfried Dead*, Künsthaus, Zürich. Fuseli was an intellectual of Swiss origin who settled in England and worked as a freelance translator and illustrator. Reynolds encouraged him to paint, and he won fame with paintings and watercolors distinguished by the originality of their themes.

dr. monro and turner

Dr. Monro's residence on Adelphi Terrace overlooking the Thames played an important role in the history of watercolor in England. Dr. Monro's hobby was painting watercolors, and when he was not busy with his career in medicine he collected paintings. He was friendly with many young watercolor artists and would try to help them out by finding buyers for their paintings or buying them himself. His collection included works by Rembrandt, Canaletto, and Lorraine, watercolors by Sandby, and paintings and sketches by Cozens and others. In 1794 he decided to open a school for watercolor artists in his own home. He bought chairs, tables, paints, brushes, and paper, and as word of his intentions quickly spread, several young artists went to him. Dr. Monro told them: "I'll pay you half a crown and give you supper for coming here every night to paint. You will learn by copying some travel notes drawn by Cozens." Dr. Monro promoted the study of Cozens's creative style and technique

Fig. 33, 34—Joseph Mallord William Turner, *The Burning of the Houses of Parliament, on the Night of October 16, 1834,* British Museum, London. (Below) *Self-Portrait,* Tate Gallery, London. Turner is, without a doubt, the best and most famous watercolor artist of England.

and kept all the paintings in his possession. A few days after the school opened, Turner, Girtin, Cotman, Cox and de Wint were busy at work. These young men later became the greatest English watercolor artists of the 18th and 19th centuries. The most able and famous of all was Joseph Mallord William Turner, followed by Thomas Girtin. According to Murray, their biographer, when they were both nineteen they went to Dr. Monro's house, where Girtin drew and Turner painted.

Turner's skill as a watercolor artist started early on. At nine he was coloring prints for a beer merchant; when he was thirteen he apprenticed with Thomas Malton, a topographer who taught him about perspective. The Royal Academy accepted one of his watercolors when he was fifteen and six years later they exhibited one of his paintings. At the young age of twenty-four he was accepted as a member of the Royal Academy, something that had never happened before to such a young artist.

turner and girtin

Fig. 35, 36—(Above) Turner, *Venice: The Grand Canal with San Simeone Piccolo at Sunset,* (Below) Turner, *Venice, St. George the Elder from the Customs House,* British Museum, London. These are two of the watercolors done by Turner on his last trip to Venice, considered the most creative paintings of all his work because of their effects of light and color.

35

36

Thomas Girtin died when he was twenty-seven years old. Together with Turner he was one of the best watercolor artists of the late 18th century. Girtin exercised considerable influence over Turner who imitated his style and use of color. When Girtin died, Turner said: "If Tom had lived I would have died of hunger."

After his experience at Monro's school in 1797, Turner began to paint in oils, alternating this medium with watercolor, which he never abandoned. He traveled to Italy four times

Fig. 37—Turner, *Scene on the Thames with Barges and a Canoe,* British Museum, London. Turner was thirty-three years old when he painted this watercolor on the banks of the Thames. In it, he shows us his ability as a draughtsman and painter, as well as his mastery over watercolor, either wet or dry. The watercolors of Venice on the previous page were painted thirteen years later.

Fig. 38—Thomas Girtin, *Kirkstall Abbey in Yorkshire,* British Museum, London. Born the same year as Turner (1775), and a classmate of his at the Monro Academy, Girtin was a reference and indispensable model for Turner and many other artists of the 18th century, consulted and imitated because of his technical and artistical merit. Thomas Girtin was one of the most important links in the development of watercolor in England.

and painted watercolors in Venice where he achieved the most creative play of light and color of his career. The French Impressionists said: "We are followers of a great master of the British school, the illustrious Turner."

bonington and cotman

Richard Parkes Bonington was an important artist in the history of English watercolor. When he was fifteen, he emigrated with his family from Nottingham to Calais, where he studied with Louis Francia, a French watercolor artist who had started out at Dr. Monro's school with Turner and Girtin. Bonington then traveled to Paris, where he learned oil painting from one of the great painters of French Romanticism, Antoine-Jean Gros. Another artist who frequented Gros's workshop and greatly admired him was Delacroix. Bonington and Delacroix, three years his senior, became friends; thus the Englishman became known to Paris Society of the time.

Jean Baptiste Camille Corot, one of the first landscape artists to paint outdoors, was struck with surprise and admiration when he saw one of Bonington's watercolor landscapes. The total range of possibilities that watercolor gave the artist had been unknown to Corot. It is therefore not exaggerating to say that Bonington spread the virtues of the watercolor medium throughout France by way of his fellow artists and their social connections. In 1825 Bonington returned to England at the same time as Delacroix. Meanwhile back in France, artists like Roqueplan and Isabey had begun to paint with watercolors following his style. The "Bonington Style" outlasted the artist, who died of tuberculosis at age twenty-seven in 1828.

John Sell Cotman deserves a special mention as "one of the best landscape artists of the 19th century in England." Cotman was also a member of the privileged few at Dr. Monro's school during the time Turner and Girtin were there. He began by imitating Girtin's style until he developed and achieved fame with his own style. It is said that Cotman advised his son who also wanted to be a painter to "draw strictly the truth; if you wish, take away or eliminate certain things, but do not add anything." Cotman was an expert in drawing and synthesis; he favored summarizing, harmonizing forms, and enriching colors, paying careful attention to the composition of the picture. He dominated the wet watercolor technique.

Figs. 39, 40—(Right) Richard Parkes Bonington, *St. Armand's Abbey in Rouen*, private collection, England. (Below) Bonington, *Venice, The Doges' Palace*, Wallace Collection, London. It is enough just to see these two watercolors to confirm the idea that Bonington was an exceptional artist. Observe, first of all, the composition, following Rembrandt's scheme, on a diagonal; note how depth is achieved by the effect of perspective; observe the idea of atmosphere or interposed space in the painting of Venice below, comparing the foreground with the diffuse and imprecise background; note the change in the color spectrum (cold spectrum above, warm below) and the inclusion of figures that, besides giving life to the paintings, serve as a reference to give a better idea of sizes and distances.

39

40

41

Fig. 41—Richard Parkes Bonington, *Venetian Scene,* Wallace Collection, London. The quality of the watercolors of Bonington, who painted landscapes just as perfectly as figures, was a decisive influence on the diffusion of watercolor painting in France, where Bonington lived for several years, associating with the major artists of the time, including Delacroix, Corot, Gros, and others.

Fig. 42—John Sell Cotman, *St Paul's Cathedral,* British Museum, London. Cotman had an instinctive sense for the art of composition and an extraordinary capacity for creating contrasts and harmonizing the colors of a painting. This, combined with his fortunate choice of subjects made him one of the best English watercolor landscape painters of the 19th century. Cotman attended Dr. Monro's academy for a time and was the most important 42 artist of the "Norwich School."

great english masters of the 19th century

John Varley and Joshua Cristall were members of the first society of watercolor painters founded in 1804. Varley was aided by Dr. Monro and became an expert in composition and color harmony. Cristall may have been somewhat more original and definitely more spontaneous.

A few years later three important artists joined the society. They were Peter de Wint, A. V. Copley Fielding, and David Cox. De Wint had been to Monro's school, where he met Girtin and studied with Varley. He was very successful painting landscapes that pictured his home region, the Lincoln plains. Copley Fielding was a master at capturing the interposed atmosphere of landscapes with lakes and mountains. His watercolors showed some resemblance to those Turner had painted earlier. David Cox was a disciple of Varley, and a very studious one at that. He wrote some books and was always trying to improve his watercolors. He tried using a new coarse grain paper and was inspired by Turner, on the latter's return from Italy, to use a richer palette.

Constable's story is different, as he usually painted with oils. He was one of Europe's best landscape artists and he experimented with gouache and watercolor.

The list of watercolor artists could be further increased by adding a group of Bonington's followers, among them Thomas Shotter Boys, William Callon, and James Holland. Other artists formed different groups throughout the 19th century. One of these groups was the Sketching Society, and its members, John Linell, Edward Calvert, George Richmond, and Samuel Palmer, were all followers of William Blake. Of this group, Samuel Palmer was the most famous. He was greatly in awe of some of Blake's work. According to Cotman's son, Palmer went through a visionary period during which he painted in a truly original and fantastic style. Another group, the Pre-Raphaelite Brotherhood, had Millais, Hunt, and the well-known Dante Gabriel Rossetti as members. They used oil paints mainly but also dabbled somewhat in watercolor. The members of the Brotherhood were grouped according to a series of precepts: painting sincerely, symbolizing ideas and subject matter, and studying iconography in depth; using bright colors, paying attention to small details; incorporating painting out of doors; and incorporating watercolor techniques. They painted medieval and biblical themes like Rossetti's famous *Ecce Ancilla Domini*.

Fig. 43—Samuel Palmer, *In a Shoreham Garden*, Victoria and Albert Museum, London. A few touches of gold and those white circular marks, painted with white gouache, are characteristic of the paintings that Palmer produced during his "Shoreham" period. He lived in Shoreham for nine years, during which he had the "dreams and visions" that unleashed his imagination.

43

44

Fig. 44—John Constable, *The Church at Stoke Poges*, Victoria and Albert Museum, London. Constable was basically a painter of oils, recognized as one of the greatest masters of English landscape painting of the 19th century. Nevertheless he occasionally painted with watercolor, in the peculiar style that can be observed in this work.

Fig. 45—David Cox (son), *The Old Church and Community of Clapham,* British Museum, London. David Cox's son, also named David, painted watercolors like his father, imitating his expert professional style, with apparent ease of technique and pleasant colors. Father and son both exhibited their works at the annual expositions held by the Royal Academy of Watercolor Artists of England.

45

Fig. 46—Peter de Wint, *Bridge Over a Tributary of the Witham River in Lincolnshire,* Tate Gallery, London. De Wint attended Dr. Monro's academy, where he met Girtin, whose influence was apparent in all his work. The plains and landscapes of Lincolnshire were his favorite subject. In the fine horizontal lines of the water and the thin blades of grass in the foreground of this watercolor, one can see lines that de Wint probably made with the end of the brush handle, using it to scratch the paint while it was still wet.

46

the success of watercolor painting in england

The success of watercolor painting can be followed chronologically.

The year 1768 marked the founding of the Royal Academy of Arts in England with Joshua Reynolds as the first president. The founding members included watercolor artists and brothers Paul and Thomas Sandby.

From the first annual exhibit held by the Academy, watercolors were exhibited. In 1804 watercolor artists, who felt discriminated against by the Academy, which deferred to works in oil paints, founded the Old Water-Colour So-

ciety. This new society held its first exhibit in 1805. Although they achieved great success, there was too much competition among members and in 1807 a rival society was founded. This group was called the Society of Painters in Miniature and Water-colours. In 1824 the Society of British Artists had as its members both oil and watercolor painters. In 1855 England sent 114 watercolors to the exhibit at the World's Fair in Paris. Both French critics and public were amazed at how well this medium had developed in England. In 1881 Queen

Figs. 47, 48—(Above) Peter de Wint, *Gloucester*, (below) John Varley, *York*, both in the British Museum, London. Two wonderful watercolors of the 19th century that would be difficult to surpass even today. Peter de Wint showed a special preference for this elongated format, which was in fashion during the first half of the 1800s. De Wint's watercolor (top) is truly tiny, measuring only 147 × 384 mm (5.8″ × 15″). John Varley's, a bit larger, is 219 × 472 mm (8.8″ × 18.6″).

49

Victoria decreed that the original (called the "Old" because it was the first) Water-Colour Society could add the word "Royal" to its title. When that Society had its first exhibit in 1805, over 12,000 paying visitors went to see it. Watercolors had achieved a clamorous success in England, a success which spread to Europe and the rest of the world.

Fig. 49—George Scharf, *The Interior of the Exposition Hall of the New Society of Painters of Watercolours*, Victoria and Albert Museum, London. The preciousness, fidelity of design, effects of light and shadow, and the feeling of atmosphere—interposed space—that Scharf achieved in this magnificent watercolor are admirable. It is a remarkably faithful reproduction of the building and ambience of this watercolor exposition mounted by the New Society of Painters of Watercolours. To understand the significance and excellence of Scharf's work, it is enough to recall that this took place in 1808—it was the second exposition held in London—and that photography did not yet exist at the time.

europe: 18th century

Watercolors were not well known in France until the late 18th century. It was only in 1775 that the French word *aquarelle* first became used as a translation, of the English "watercolor." There was, however, a French artist, Hubert Robert, whose watercolors had been well received by the critics and the public. In 1754, Robert went to Rome and spent eleven years in Italy. He studied with Piranesi and Panini, painting landscapes with ruins. He was accompanied briefly by another French artist, Fragonard, in 1761. Two other Frenchmen, Desprez and Challe, also went to Rome to paint *vedutas*. The activities of these artists helped to promote watercolor painting in France.

Switzerland, land of fascinating landscapes, gave us outstanding artists such as Johan Ludwig Aberli and Abraham Louis Rodolphe Ducros. Aberli was a bucolic artist and a nature lover. Ducros used such powerful contrast and intensity in his watercolors that at first sight they seemed to be painted in oils. He worked with a reduced range of colors, made up mainly of ochres, siennas, and blues. It is possible that during his stay in Rome his style influenced the English watercolor painters.

An interesting theme of 18th-century art is that of botanical paintings. One of the best-known artists was Pierre Joseph Redoute, who was born in Ardennes. In Holland we can admire Jan Van Huysum and his follower Gerard Van Spaendock.

50

51

Fig. 50—Abraham Louis Rodolphe Ducros, *Night Storm in Cefalou, Calabria,* Cantonal Museum of Fine Arts, Lausanne. With a limited spectrum of colors—ochre, sienna, and blue—Ducros achieved this spectacular richness of color that even fooled the experts into thinking that this was an oil painting. Ducros also demonstrated a magnificent talent for construction and drawing, enabling the artist to sell his etchings easily while he was in Italy.

Figs. 51, 52—(Left) Gerard Van Spaëndonck, *Campsis Radicaus,* (right) Jan Van Huysum, *Study of Flowers in a Vase,* Fitzwilliam Museum, Cambridge, England.

52

Fig. 53—Johann Ludwig Aberli, *The Waterfall,* Victoria and Albert Museum, London. In this watercolor, painted around 1750, one can still note the style associated with *vedutas* or etchings in the definition of forms by fine penstrokes or intense color. This formula which made it possible to "fill in" etchings done in a series by painting in, is less obvious here thanks to Aberli's skill. He controlled the contrasts between foreground and background in order to create the so-called aerial perspective or illusion of interposed atmosphere. These same effects can be seen in the reproduction of the watercolor by Paul Sandby in fig. 29.

53

europe: 19th century

During the early part of the 19th century, Ingres was against Delacroix and vice versa. Jean Auguste Dominique Ingres was a staunch believer in Classicism, Raphael, academic painting, and maintaining the status quo in art. On the other hand, Eugène Delacroix was the leader of Romanticism and opened the doors for Realism, Impressionism, and Modern Art. Delacroix emerged victorious and his success became that of watercolor as well. Nineteenth-century art grew in the direction of greater color, synthesis, and light, and a brighter palette. In essence, watercolor art is color, synthesis, and light.

Because of his ideas Ingres painted few watercolors, while Delacroix was an ardent watercolor artist. He was Bonington's friend and visited London, Rome, and North Africa. In the latter he painted numerous watercolors depicting typical scenes and people.

Outstanding in France were Paul Gavarni and Eugene Lami. The latter founded the Société d'Aquarellistes in 1879. Founding members included Gustave Doré, Isabey, and Harpignies. It is well known that Honoré Daumier used watercolor to illuminate his political cartoons. It is surprising to learn that, except for Berthe Morisot and Eugene Boudin, the Impressionists did not use watercolors. (Cézanne is a separate case.) Lastly there is the painter and teacher Gustave Moreau, whose pupils included Roualt, Matisse, and Marquet.

The Dutchman Johan Bar Thold Jongkind painted marvelous watercolors as well as oil paintings. He spent a great part of his life in Paris and, with Boudin, became a prime supporter of the Impressionist movement.

Watercolors became appreciated in Germany during the second half of the 19th century. Among the well-known artists are Johann Lucas Von Hildebrandt and Adolf von Menzel. Scotsman David Robert took watercolor art to Spain where it caught on thanks to the enthusiasm of Perez Villaamil. The pair traveled with the new art throughout the Iberian peninsula. Two excellent watercolor artists, Lucas and Algarra, collaborated with Villaamil. It was Mariano Fortuny, however, who made watercolor better known throughout Spain. He was one of the best artists of the 18th century and had a great knowledge of the procedures that watercolor involved.

Mariano Fortuny, born in Reus, in the province of Tarragona, but who had his own studio in Barcelona, was, furthermore, the instigator of the first Spanish association of

54

55

Fig. 54—Eugène Delacroix, *Horse Attacked by a Panther,* Louvre, Paris. Quick notes, like sketches, on subjects in his imagination or painted from nature, were a constant occupation and exercise for Delacroix. The tens of hundreds of notes that he did during his trips—drawings of animals or subjects in the countries he visited—were almost always done in watercolors.

Fig. 55—Johan Barthold Jongkind, *Dutch Harbor,* Fine Arts Museum, Budapest. Pupil of Isabey and born in Holland, he spent most of his time in Paris, where he studied under Isabey and mixed with the Impressionists. Jongkind worked with oil paint as well as with watercolors, specializing in maritime subjects characterized by their precise drawing.

watercolor painters, which was founded in 1864, in Barcelona, under the name of Centre d'Aquarel·listes. From this emerged, first in 1881 the Cercle Artistic and later in 1920, the present Agrupació d'Aquarel·listes de Catalunya. At the national level, the first association called Sociedad de Acuarelistas was founded in Madrid in 1878.

Fig. 56—Eugène-Louis Lami, *Louis XIV in the Gardens of Versailles*, Louvre, Paris. Lami was an expert in watercolor. His good relations with the upper class of the French Second Empire allowed him to join the court and specialize in subjects like this one, inspired by French history.

56

Fig. 57—Henri Harpignies, *View of the Seine with the Tuileries*, Louvre, Paris. Contemporary of such illustration and watercolor experts as Ciceri, Lami, Gavarni, Daumier and Doré, Harpignies is one of the most renowned French watercolor painters of the last century, remarkable for the soberness of his colors and the perfection of his drawing.

57

mariano fortuny

Fig. 58—Mariano Fortuny y Carbo, *Half-naked Man*, Goya Museum, Castres. Fortuny was an all-round artist. He drew with great ease; he left oil paintings which exhibit a control over the figure that won him the surname of "master;" and he used watercolors with truly remarkable craftsmanship. He went to Rome when he was twenty. After two years of study he traveled to Morocco where he produced the official commission of ten big paintings about the Spanish-Moroccan war. In Morocco he made several watercolors, including the one reproduced here. Then came trips to Paris, London, Rome again, Granada, Rome... Unfortunately, Fortuny died at the age of thirty-six, considered among the greatest watercolor artists of the 19th century.

58

cézanne

Fig. 59—Paul Cézanne, *Boy with Red Coat*. Walter Filechenfeldt Collection, Zurich. Without doubt, Cézanne is modern, contemporary. Between Mariano Fortuny's painting on the previous page, made around 1862, and Cézanne's work of 1902, some forty years have passed. What a jump, what a radical change! During those forty years, Impressionism was born, the palette was purged, shape and color were resumed, details lost their importance. Cézanne went beyond Impressionism: he embodied Post-Impressionism, and laid the foundations of Cubism. He is credited today as one of the great promoters of modern painting. This watercolor confirms this: it could have been painted today, in the late 20th century.

59

europe in the first half of the 20th century

The first abstract painting in the history of art was a watercolor painted in 1910 by Wassily Kandinsky.

However, watercolor artists, with a few exceptions, did not participate in this art form. As a matter of fact they kept their distance from the styles and movements that came in rapid succession during the first half of the 20th century. They did, however, incorporate into their works the light and spontaneity of the Impressionists and use the colors and contrasts and some new schemes of composition from Modern Art in general.

On the other hand, the great masters of Modern Art, Picasso, Dali, Miró, Matisse, and Braque, hardly ever used watercolor. In spite of this the quantity and quality of watercolor artists throughout Europe grew to such proportion that it becomes difficult for us to single out any one here. There are, however, certain important innovations that bear mentioning. There was a tendency to use watercolor to imitate oil paint, using greater body and color and sacrificing transparency. Anther innovation was the use of "tricks" such as using wax or masking fluid to set off open spaces or using

60

turpentine, salt, stains, or sprayguns to achieve special effects.

On this page you can see some watercolors from the early 20th century. They include works by Wassily Kandinsky, the artist of the first abstract mentioned earlier, Emil Nolde, and August Macke. On the next page we see works by Maurice de Vlaminck, Maurice Utrillo, Juan Gris, and Pablo Picasso. These are all well-known artists who, except for Nolde, did not usually work in watercolors.

Fig. 60—Wassily Kandinsky, *The Cossacks*, Tate Gallery, London. A watercolor similar to this was the first abstract painting, painted in watercolors by Kandinsky in the year 1910.

Fig. 61—Emil Nolde, *Irises and Poppies*, Ada and Emil Nolde Foundation. Nolde was a German Expressionist painter who felt a great passion for primitive art and nature.

Fig. 62—August Macke, *Yellow Jake*, Ulmer Museum, Ulm. In this watercolor, Macke offers us a sample of his Futuristic style and his Post-Impressionist coloring, both factors directly influenced by Delaunay, who with Kandinsky and Macke formed part of the Blaue Reiter (Blue Rider) group.

63

65

64

66

Fig. 63—Maurice de Vlaminck, *Landscape,* Staatsgalerie, Stuttgart. Matisse, together with Derain, Vlaminck, and other artists, were the initiators, along with an exposition held in Paris in 1905, of the tendency or style called *Fauvism* (wild beasts). This title, first applied by an art critic, described a way of painting with violent colors and contrasts. However, after two or three years, Vlaminck stopped painting like a Fauve and drew closer to the theories and style of Cézanne.

Fig. 64—Maurice Utrillo, *The Rue Sainte-Rustique Covered in Snow,* Paul Petrides Collection, Paris. This watercolor with a mixture of white gouache, is typical of Utrillo's style: an innocent, childlike way of drawing and painting, appropriately called "the difficult innocence."

Fig. 65—Juan Gris, *Three Lamps,* Museum of Fine Arts, Berne. Between 1909 and 1910 the Spanish painter Juan Gris did some watercolor paintings to practice drawing forms and color. Apparently, what Gris was trying to determine with these oversized studies —47.8×61.8 cm (19″×24″)— was what direction to follow in the future. In fact, a year later, together with his friends Picasso and Braque, he started on the adventure of Cubism.

Fig. 66—Pablo Picasso, *Young Acrobat and Child,* Guggenheim Museum, New York. This is one of the many sketches that Picasso did for the painting *Trapeze Artists (Family of Saltimbanques),* just as he was in transition between his blue and pink periods. This is a watercolor with a mixture of gouache.

watercolor painting today

On this page and the ones that follow you will see some contemporary watercolors whose form and color reveal a language in harmony with today's art. While some are impressionist and others expressionist, they are linked by the constructive base watercolor painters have never abandoned.

Watercolors still depict traditional topics: country landscapes, seascapes, ports, railroads, still lifes, portraits and figures, and nature in general. Present-day scenes, such as urban areas and suburban houses and streets, are also represented.

67

68

Fig. 67—André Dunoyer de Segonzac, *Feucherolles in Autumn,* private collection. Segonzac was primarily an Impressionist, influenced by Cézanne, who also did many etchings—1,500 of them from 1919 onward—which are today considered his best works.

Fig. 68—Roland Oudot, *La Giudecca, Venice,* Albert Balser Collection, Geneva. Roland Oudot's style draws our attention by its emphasis on the drawing, with the forms outlined with a fine line of India ink. The coloring is also characteristic of his style, with the shadowed areas where blues, siennas, grays, and reds interact with a vibration that undoubtedly gives quality to the work.

Fig. 69—Emilio Grausala, *Venice,* private collection. Grausala, a Catalan painter, moved to Paris in 1932 and became a part of the Second Spanish School of Paris, as it was called. He generally painted with oils, but on some trips and in private he did small watercolor works painted with his proverbial gaiety and richness of color.

69

Fig. 70—Ives Brayer, *Flower Market, Mexico,* This work represents a modern concept of watercolor painting: a synthesis of form and color, explaining the subject in an abbreviated manner without entering into details; a premeditated luminosity with a predominance of light colors over dark; and a richness of colors, also calculated to add to the transparency typical of watercolor. Brayer always paints with watercolor. He draws with great mastery, usually with lead pencil, and he always works with the model in front of him.

70

watercolor painting today

Fig. 71.—Ives Brayer. *Half-light at Baux-de-Provence,* private collection. As can be seen in this landscape, Brayer painted with conventional colors, attentive to the realism offered by the scene, attempting to capture the first impression suggested by the subject, applying pure watercolor techniques, enjoying "the pleasure of playing with the white of the paper"—as he puts it himself—*"en utilisant juste une coulée de couleur, du bout du pinceau"* (sic).

Fig. 72—John Piper, *Bethesda, North Wales,* private collection. Piper is known as an excellent modern interpreter of the British landscape, which he rendered with an obvious mastery of technique and medium. In this landscape for instance, he mixed watercolors with India ink, layering wet over wet, and using *frottis,* the dry brush technique. A book of his work done in England and Wales was recently published.

71

72

73

74

Fig. 73.—Julio Quesada, *Landscape; Tamajón (Guadalajara)*, private collection. This is an excellent example of contemporary watercolors, as the Spanish artist, Julio Quesada, is so capable of exemplifying. He paints in his own way, with a very personal vision and interpretation; with a sober but perfectly harmonized color scheme; synthesizing, summarizing in a few exact, precise brushstrokes, which nevertheless capture the forms, the site, the fields, and the trees. But above all, he executes all this with an exceptional mastery of pure watercolor technique.

Fig. 74—Michel Ciry, *Segovia*, private collection, Lausanne. Michel Ciry decided to paint watercolors around 1960. Six years later, he obtained these results while painting in central Spain. In harmony with the Castilian landscape, Ciry paints with a subdued, warm palette, formed of ochres, siennas, and grays, interrupting the landscape with houses and roads that contrast with the black trees and the earth scorched by the sun. This painting is a good example of the synthesis of form and color.

the 19th and 20th centuries in the united states

The American Watercolor Society was formed in 1866 with Samuel Colman as its president.

At that time watercolor was already popular in the United States. This was mainly because oil painters Thomas Eakins and Winslow Homer also used watercolor. Homer was a bohemian loner who worked as a magazine illustrator, correspondent, and sketcher. During his travels he visited France, England, Canada, Bermuda, and Nassau. After the age of forty, he devoted himself entirely to painting. He had a special gift for choosing marine landscapes and then painting them with oils or watercolors and giving them extraordinary color.

The end of the 19th century was a marvelous time for American watercolor. Maurice Prendergast depicted groups of people. Mary Cassatt lived the adventure of Impressionism in France. James Abott McNeill Whistler was also an Impressionist. John Singer Sargent, the famous portrait and watercolor artist, though American, was born in Italy and educat-

75

Fig. 75—Maurice Prendergast, *Low Tide, Beachmont,* Worchester Art Museum. Born in Boston, Prendergast went to Paris at the age of twenty-one when Impressionism was in full swing, so it is not strange that his paintings should be influenced by Manet, Monet, Renoir, Pissarro, etc. Curiously, Prendergast specialized in the subject of crowds, or groups of people in a particular situation, as in his painting *The Walk,* or in this one, *Low Tide.* In 1914, he returned from Europe to New York, where he exhibited with Los Pocho, a radical group that indirectly infused American art with new life.

76

Fig. 76—John Singer Sargent, *Mountain Stream*, Metropolitan Museum of Art, New York. Painting his magnificent portraits in oils, Sargent was fabulous; painting with watercolors he was also extraordinary. At eighteen he was in Paris studying under the painter Carolus, who inculcated him with a basic rule on synthesis that became Sargent's credo during his career as an artist: "In art, anything that is not indispensable is prejudicial."

Fig. 77—Edward Hopper, *The Mansard Roof*, Brooklyn Museum, New York. When Hopper visited Paris at the age of twenty-four, he was influenced by Post-Impressionism, but upon his return to America, he shook off this influence to take up American Realism and specialize in urban scenes. In this watercolor, painted with admirable skill in the year 1923, Hopper cannot be defined as to style, but he gives us an excellent lesson on the effects of light and shadow, volume, color, and watercolor technique.

77

d in France. These four artists took the reins nd led American art to its glorious finish at he end of the century.

During our century, watercolor painting has chieved first place in the United States. It has housands of fans and highly qualified artists oo numerous to mention. We can cite a few xamples to show how high the standards re. Figurative art is represented by Edward Hopper, Andrew Wyeth, Rowland Hilder, ohn Pike, and David Millard. The modern nd even abstract styles are represented y John Marin, Georgia O'Keeffe, Lyonel Feininger, and Sam Francis.

History continues. Watercolor now has a place s a highly expressive medium. It has reached level of quality and quantity that can be ompared only with oil painting. The trends urrently being followed with new techniques nd styles could make watercolor painting ven more exciting.

Fig. 78—Charles Reid, *Masculine Figure, Clothed*, private collection. I have chosen this watercolor by Reid as representative of a large number of amateur and professional artists who are presently painting watercolors in the United States and of the quality of these American watercolorists. As can be seen, Reid is a great watercolor artist, and he has published several books on art and creativity.

78

79

Fig. 79—Federico Lloveras, *Alta-fulla, Tarragona,* private collection. To conclude this brief history of watercolor, I choose this simple landscape by my friend Federico Lloveras, recently deceased. He was a great artist of worldwide reknown, who had painted in every corner of Spain, and all the cities of Europe and America. All his watercolors illustrated the ease with which he painted, as does the one shown here, which, characteristically, seems so simple, at first view. In an interview with Mr. del Arco for *La Vanguardia,* he was asked how he managed to create this freshness, this feeling of "a watercolor painted in just a few minutes." Lloveras answered: "I see a theme: I spend a lot of time studying, observing. Then I begin to paint—without hurry, very slowly, trying out, then hesitating. Because at first the subject dominates you, and you have to fight so that you dominate the subject. Once this happens, I can work securely; I know where and how to place every brushstroke. And then it seems as if I had painted the picture in a moment."

the painter's
studio

"A small room captures the spirit; one should paint by the light of one window."

Leonardo da Vinci (1452-1519)

the studio for painting in watercolor

The watercolor artist usually works outdoors. His favorite subjects are usually landscapes, seascapes, city streets and squares. Nevertheless the watercolorist, like the painter of oils, also needs a studio for drawing, painting from sketches, still lifes, figures from nature, portraits...

To begin all you need is a tabletop easel and another table to hold water pitchers, brushes and paints, a sketch pad, a chair, a desk lamp, and a pair of portfolios in which you can store drawing paper and finished works.

The studio of many professionals is as barren as the one mentioned earlier. However, if one wants to invest in setting up a place to work very comfortably the following would be an excellent choice:

A room measuring 4 m square (about 12 square feet) with white walls and large windows with a northern exposure for working in daylight. A good choice for a table would be one whose top can be tilted at different angles. The chair should have an upholstered seat and back, at a height that can be adjusted at will and metal casters for easier rolling. To keep supplies, such as pitchers of water and the box

Fig. 81—The amateur, to begin, can install his studio in any room in the house. All that is needed is a table, a drawing board, and a chair. The board allows the artist to hold the watercolor paper at a slight incline by resting the board on the table with the help of a few books, or at a greater slant by resting it in his lap and against the edge of the table.

81

82

Fig. 82—Sir William Orpen, *The Model,* Tate Gallery, London. The Irishman Sir William Orpen offers us, in this magnificent watercolor, a partial view of his studio in London, apparently a small one to judge by this 1911 painting.

lighting the professional studio

83

of watercolors close by, it is useful to have an auxiliary table, also on casters. To paint you need a studio easel and a tabletop easel. A bookshelf wall unit with drawers is a useful place to put away paper, sketches, first drafts, and the end product. A stand for file folders, a sink with running water, art books, a stereo, and a sofa or loveseat where your model can sit or where you can listen to music, read, or chat with friends are also nice to have.

The main source of daylight should come from large windows to the left of the work table. It is wise to have blinds or curtains since they allow you to regulate the amount and type of light. Your electrical lighting should be powerful and evenly distributed, allowing the use of the studio for painting at night. It is wise to consult with an electrician and install at least one lamp with four fluorescent bulbs. Two of these should give warm light and two cold light to imitate natural daylight. A table lamp should have an extendable arm and give off at least 100 watts. Finally, it is important to have light near the sofa and create an intimate spot for relaxing, listening to music, and talking.

84

Fig. 83—Gaspar Romero's studio in his house in Barcelona. As you can see, the furniture is limited to a folding table with a slanted top, a small side table, a studio easel of the classic three-legged type, and a stool for working partially seated.

Fig. 84—This is an ideal studio for watercolor painting: a room with white walls, 4 × 4 m (12' × 12'), with large windows facing north and the following furniture and lighting:

Furniture and tools

1: Table. 2: Tabletop easel in the form of a lectern. 3: Auxiliary table with wheels. 4: Swivel chair, with adjustable height and wheels. 5: Bookshelf. 6: Counter with tray-drawers. 7: Set of drawers above the counter to store materials. 7a: White glass with electrical fixture inside the top drawer, for trading designs, looking at slides, etc. 8: Stereo equipment. 9: Sink or basin with running water (not shown in figure).
Lighting. A: Windows, daylight. B: Set of Fluorescent lights. C: Table lamp. D: auxiliary lamp.

furniture and tools

The following is a list of the furnishings necessary for the studio of a professional watercolor artist.

A table for painting. This can be a regular office desk with drawers to keep boxes, brushes, and other materials. However, this type of table is only a temporary solution. Professionally speaking, it is best to work with a table designed specifically for drawing.

An inclined tabletop allows for a better view of the painting currently being worked on. For this purpose, please look at the classical folding table (fig. 86) which has been on the market for over fifty years. This style is known to young and old watercolor artists, but it has been outdated by more modern and functional designs. Modern tables include those used for technical drawing and architectural drafting, which are also useful for artistic drawing and painting. They are made of formica with metal hardware and have functional designs and elegant lines (figs. 87, 89). The latter, custom-made, has two independent sets of drawers and a slanted tabletop. This allows for the drawers to be separated and the table size to be increased on both sides. Please note in the same figure that the depth of the drawers

85

Fig. 85—These are the pieces of furniture that are really indispensable for working in the watercolor studio: the regular drawing table, a lectern-type tabletop easel, a small side table, and a comfortable swivel chair with wheels and adjustable height. Paints, brushes, jars with water, paper, etc.

Fig. 86—The classic drafting table with a top that can be slanted as desired—in use for over a hundred years—is still found in the studios of many professional watercolorists.

Fig. 87—The modern table, like this "pioneer" by the maker Americana, in the United States, can be both elegant and functional, as seen in this picture. It has a top that can be tilted at any angle, drawers for extra materials, bars to rest the feet on, and other features.

86

87

llows for a board to be placed on one of them to form an auxiliary table. This will substitute for the second table mentioned earlier as a place to put water, brushes and colors. Other necessary objects include a table-top easel like the one seen in fig. 85 and a classical three-legged easel.

It is necessary to have a smaller table on which to place water, paper, brushes, sponges, and paper towels. This can be a special piece of furniture with springs, shelves, and all kinds of drawers. If it also has a tilted board it is possible to paint without any table (fig. 86). It is even possible to use a normal table or a contraption such as the one I use. This consists of a regular typing table with a board on top (fig. 90). Regardless of the style you choose, this second table should have casters or wheels. This way it can be easily transported to the drawing table or easel you are currently using.

A professional studio also needs a stand like the one in fig. 91 on which one or two large portfolios with sketches or finished paintings can be left. This makes it easier to show your work to visitors and prospective buyers.

88

Fig. 88—Here is a marvelous invention that combines in a single piece of furniture the table, tabletop easel, a shelf that serves as an auxiliary table, two shelves to store materials, and three tray-drawers to keep paper, drawings, and watercolors (maximum size 32 × 50 cm). Equipped with wheels, it is at the very least a complete auxiliary table.

Fig. 89—Drawing table formed by two sets of drawers and a separate board as the desk top, allowing the table to be lengthened by moving the drawers out. The drawers are long enough so that one of them can be used as an auxiliary table by placing a board on top of it.

Fig. 90—Some time ago, using an old typewriter table and a simple wooden board that I tied to the table, I made this sort of auxiliary table on wheels, which works just as well for oil painting as for watercolor.

89

90

91

Fig. 91—The stand for large portfolios that the artist uses for keeping paper and completed work is essential in a studio, both to conserve the pieces and to show them to friends and clients.

running water, wall unit, armchair...

Running water in the studio is not a must, but it does make life more comfortable. You will need water to paint and it has to be changed periodically. The reason why the source of water should be close by is because you also need it to wash the palette, the box, the brushes, and other things. You can also use it as part of the normal white sink with chrome faucet. I installed one made of traditional ceramic and the result is quite pleasing.

If the studio is large enough, a complete wall unit may be a worthwhile investment. You can use the regular drawers to put away brushes, colors, palette, and jars. Tray-type drawers are the best place to keep your paper, future pro-

jects, sketches, drawings, and finished watercolors. This unit should also have a table with a large enough surface to fold, cut, and mount the paper.

You will need to have two or three boards with a depth of 6 mm and two standard measures, about 85 × 60 cm and 100 × 70 cm.

I recommend that you have a comfortable chair. It should be on casters with upholstered arms and back and adjustable height, similar to those used in offices. Painting is a tiring procedure. Do not forget that inspiration and creativity are still on speaking terms with comfort.

92

Fig. 92—Running water is needed in a studio, but instead of an ordinary sink and faucet, I installed this decorative basin of old-fashioned porcelain at very little extra cost.

Fig. 93—You can work in your studio with the traditional round wooden three-legged stool, but I recommend drawing and painting on a comfortable swivel chair with adjustable height and wheels. You'll see that it's worth it

Fig. 94—There should be at least two large sturdy portfolios in the studio and two or three 6 mm (1/4") thick plywood boards, two of them 65 × 80 cm (26" × 32") and one 70 × 100 mm (28" × 40").

Fig. 95—Notice this piece of furniture, with one section serving as a bookshelf and another as a counter, and tray-drawers to store blank paper, sketches, designs, and original watercolors that are finished or in progress. A set of drawers can be added to this table to store materials and tools. One of the top drawers can be fitted with a clouded glass with two fluorescent lamps inside the drawer and used as a tracing table, or for looking at slides, etc.

93

94

95

materials and tools

the easel

Most easels used in oil painting are also useful for watercolor painting. There are some like the tabletop easel that have been designed specifically with the watercolor artist in mind. Every easel for watercolors needs a supplementary wooden board to hold the paper. This is not necessary if the paper is attached to a board or rigid block made especially for painting in watercolor.

Among professionals there is no set or agreed-upon angle at which their drawing pad should be tilted. Some work outdoors with the board lying flat on the ground; others prefer the aid of an easel for tilting the board the way they want it. Indoors the situation is similar; some work on their desk which is slightly tilted, others use a tabletop easel set at a 45° angle, while there are those that use a conventional easel, which places their work perpendicular to the floor. It is my belief that a 45° angle is the most appropriate for developing adequate watercolor techniques.

A good portable easel for working outdoors should meet the following requirements: lightweight, stable, movable height, and a mechanism to hold the paper in its place.

Fig. 97—Special tabletop easel for watercolor painting. The design is almost identical to that of a traditional studio easel like the one shown in fig. 103, with the exception of its smaller size of 60 cm. It can be tilted at any angle, for painting in a vertical position or at a greater or lesser slant.

Fig. 99—A portable metal, folding easel, highly recommended for watercolor painting because of its compact solid mechanism that makes it possible to slant the arm (A) as desired, to hold the board or pad of paper firmly in place.

Fig. 100—Portable easel for watercolor painting, made of wood, similar to the one in fig. 99, also foldable, but with the addition of a small board on which the watercolor palette can be placed. The inclined arm (A) of this model is not as sturdy or steady as the one on the previous easel.

Fig. 101—Traditional easel with its own case, in common use in Europe and America for oil or watercolor painting. The top can be slanted as desired, and all the materials and tools needed for watercolor painting can be carried in the case. This stylized model is slightly narrower and lighter than the standard model.

Fig. 102—Traditional studio easel with a tripod and an adjustable height tray, but smaller than the traditional model for oil painting.

Figs. 103, 104—Studio easel that can be used for oil or watercolor painting thanks to its slanting top. It is solidly and functionally built, and takes up less space than the traditional studio easel (fig. 104 shows it folded).

Fig. 105—Finally, this is the best known and most commonly used studio easel for oil painting. It can also be used for water color painting provided the board is in a vertical position, though this may not really be advisable.

A

100

99

101

Fig. 98—Tabletop easel designed for watercolor painting. It has the form of a lectern and can be tilted to 45°. Whether painting watercolors with this or any other type of easel, a board is needed on which to rest or fasten the paper, unless you are painting with paper mounted on cardboard or on a drawing tablet.

97

98

102

103

104

105

paper for watercolor painting

In watercolor painting the choice of the right paper is very important. There is paper made of wood pulp which is made by machines or molds, and has a medium quality. Papers of the best quality contain a 100% rag and are handmade with great care given to how they are glued. This last process determines the paper's quality and how it will stand up to the many layers of watercolor applied. The highest-quality paper is quite expensive but there is an intermediate quality made by some companies that is acceptable. High-quality papers can be distinguished by the mark of the manufacturer somewhere on the paper either stamped in relief, or the traditional watermark, which can be better observed by holding the paper up to a light.

There are three basic textures of paper that are suitable for watercolors:

A) Fine-grain paper

B) Medium-grain paper or semirough

C) Coarse-grain paper or rough

Fine-grain paper is pressed while hot to straighten it. However, it does maintain certain ridges that are needed for watercolor to adhere. This is why a completely flat paper is not well suited for this art form. Fine-grain paper is very good for drawing and painting with watercolor if the artist is an expert at controlling outlines, fusions, gradations, and wet contours, since the finer the grain the faster the paint will slide and dry. Although this is not an easy paper to work with, it does increase the luminosity of colors. Medium-grain paper has ridges which make it unnecessary to work at very fast speeds. Its spot, right in the middle between the most difficult and the easiest paper, makes it ideal for the beginner. This person should wait a while before trying other grains of paper.

Coarse-grain paper prepared for watercolor painting offers an accentuated degree of small holes dispersed regularly but asymmetrically throughout the paper. These holes retain and accumulate the wet watercolor paint so that it takes longer for them to dry. These holes make it difficult for the beginner to work with watercolor. However, for the professional, they offer a better control of moisture and of the watercolor paints themselves. In theory this paper takes away the brilliance associated with watercolor because each hole acts as a miniature shadow. However, in practice this darkening of the painting is hardly perceptible. All these papers have a front and a back which should be taken into account because the front has a better finish. The easiest way to know which side is which is that the grain in front is asymmetric while on the back the grain has a more regular texture and can even form a small design or diagonal pattern.

Fig. 106—To distinguish between drawing paper and good quality watercolor paper, machine or man-made, manufacturers stamp their dry mark in relief in one of the sheet's corners, or they print their logo with the traditional watermark, which can be seen by holding the paper up to the light. (A list of internationally known manufacturers of drawing or watercolor paper appears on the next page.)

10€

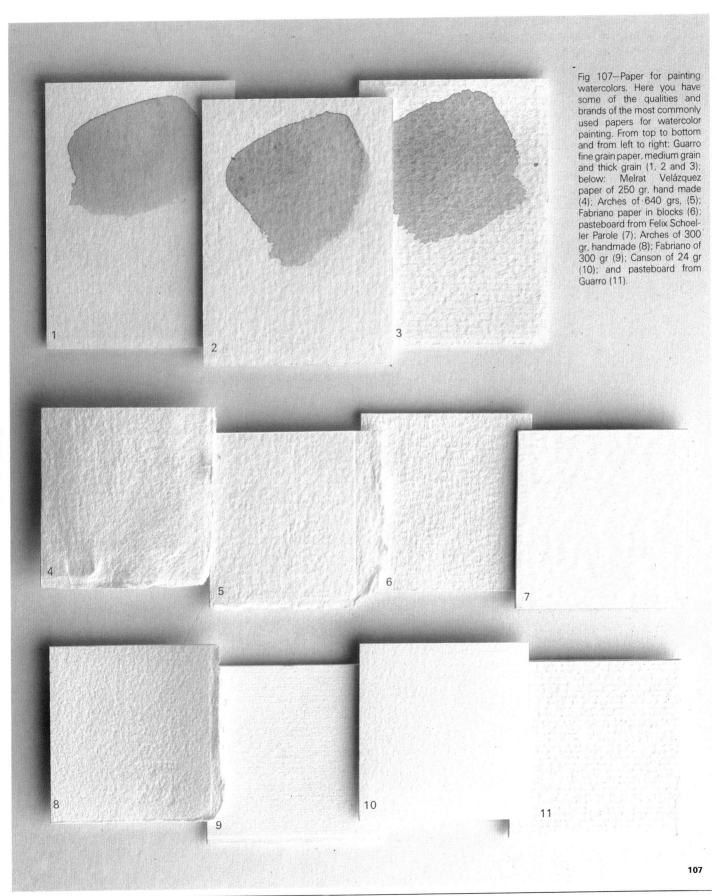

Fig 107—Paper for painting watercolors. Here you have some of the qualities and brands of the most commonly used papers for watercolor painting. From top to bottom and from left to right: Guarro fine grain paper, medium grain and thick grain (1, 2 and 3); below: Melrat Velázquez paper of 250 gr, hand made (4); Arches of 640 grs, (5); Fabriano paper in blocks (6); pasteboard from Felix Schoeller Parole (7); Arches of 300 gr, handmade (8); Fabriano of 300 gr (9); Canson of 24 gr (10); and pasteboard from Guarro (11).

107

paper for watercolor painting

The unit used for measuring paper is the ream, which is 500 sheets, regardless of their size. The weight of the ream and its conversion to grams per square meter of paper determine how thick the paper actually is. We therefore have very light paper of 45 grams, cardboard of 370 grams, and other sizes in between.

You can buy paper in single sheets of specific measurements. Papers also come mounted on cardboard to eliminate the possibility of warping produced by the moisture of the watercolor paints and water. This paper is usually found in blocks of 20 or 25 sheets, glued to one another by all four corners, thus forming a compact unit that keeps its shape while one is painting.

Watercolor papers come in a large selection of sizes, from pads small enough to stick in your pocket, to large sheets for landscape painting. These sizes differ from country to country according to individual manufacturers. England has six different sizes from the small Royal Half (381 × 559 mm) to the large Antiquarium (787 × 1346 mm).

MANUFACTURERS OF QUALITY PAPER FOR USE IN WATERCOLOR PAINTING

Arches
Grumbacher
Strathmore
Winslow
Winsor & Newton
Watchung
R.W.S. (Royal Watercolour Society)
Guarro
Canson & Montgolfier
Fabriano
Scholler Parole
Whatman

Fig. 108—Drawing paper or watercolor paper is sold in individual sheets, in sheets attached to cardboard, or in pads. Some of this paper has the irregular edges that indicate it is handmade. Other sheets have regular, even edges, an indication that they are machine-cut. Watercolor paper is also sold glued to thick, sturdy cardboard, eliminating the need to mount it on a board or use a back-up board. Drawing and watercolor papers are not, unfortunately, made in universally accepted standard sizes. But there is a great variety of sizes available to suit your needs and preferences.

Fig. 109—Most paper manufacturers make pads of 20 or 25 sheets attached to a thick piece of cardboard and "bound" with plastic glue on all four sides, forming a compact block with the sheets taut, thus eliminating the problems of curling or warping caused by the moisture of the paints.

stretching the paper

How to stretch the paper over the wooden board: To paint on a sheet as taut as a drum, without ripples, creases, or puckers caused by the watercolor's moisture, follow this procedure:

Fig. 110—Take the sheet of watercolor paper in both hands and hold it under running water, wetting it completely for about two minutes.

Fig. 111—Transfer the soaked paper immediately to a board, and while it is still wet, stretch it a bit with both hands.

Fig. 112—Immediately, without delay, tape one of the edges with a strip of gummed tape (paper on a roll 2 to 3 cm—or 3/4'' to 1'' wide).

Fig. 113—Continue to tape all four sides of the sheet of paper with gummed tape and then leave everything to dry, keeping the board and paper in a horizontal position, without trying to speed the drying process with mechanical or forced means (in the sun, with dryers or heaters, etc.). After four or five hours, when the paper is dry, you will be able to paint on a smooth, taut surface that will not wrinkle no matter how much water your paints require.

Fig. 114—The paper can also be stretched by moistening it and fastening it with metal staples from a staple gun such as decorators use.

Fig. 115—We should add, finally, that thanks to the remarkable thickness of watercolor papers sold today by most manufacturers, many professional artists skip stretching their paper and simply fasten it down with thumbtacks or metal clips, without wetting it first.

If you paint on paper weighing less than 200 grams per square meter, you will find that the wetness of the watercolor will make the paper warp. To avoid this you must first mount and tense the paper. This is done by wetting the paper under the water faucet and allowing it to stretch on a tabletop for a short while. Then the paper should be taped so that, as it dries and shrinks, it will remain flat and tense and not be affected by water.

In practice, however, most professionals skip the above-mentioned steps because they work with cardboardlike paper or with a block of mounted paper. Both of these eliminate the problems of warping. A professional friend of mine said: "We hardly ever use the method of wetting the paper and taping it to a board. I just thumbtack the paper and it is ready."

For those perfectionists who always like to use the correct methods, we present with figures and text the most frequently used methods of mounting watercolor paper.

114

115

watercolor colors

The colors used in watercolor painting are vegetable, mineral, or animal pigments mixed together with water and gum arabic. Honey and glycerine are added to prevent thick coats of paint from cracking as they dry, and a preservative is added to keep the paint fresh longer. You can find paint in these four types:

Tablets of dry watercolors

Tablets of moist watercolors

Tubes of creamy watercolors

Jars of liquid watercolors

The tablets of dry watercolors are usually associated with an inexpensive product. They come in round button-like shapes and you have to use your brush firmly to obtain color from them.

The tablets of moist watercolors are of professional quality and come in white plastic square boxes. To make the wet watercolors, the manufacturer increases the amounts of honey and glycerine and uses pigments of higher quality so the colors dilute faster.

Moist watercolors come in metallic boxes with 6, 12, or 24 tablets, but they can also be bought individually.

Creamy watercolors in tubes are also of professional quality.

They dilute instantaneously in water and give the same transparency as moist colors in tablets. They are available in boxes of 6 and 12 tubes and the ones with a capacity of 8 cm³ are the most popular. You can also buy refill tubes.

Lastly we have liquid watercolors, which come in crystal jars. They are commonly used by illustrators and to a lesser extent in artistic watercolor painting to resolve backgrounds or graduated washes.

The professional artist uses both moist watercolors in tablets and creamy watercolors in tubes. It is difficult to choose or give advice as to which one is the best. I think it depends on skill and what one is accustomed to. The finished product will be the same.

Fig. 116—Pans of dry watercolors of an inexpensive type. These come in palette boxes with six or twelve colors. Some makers supply individual refills for separate colors.

116

Fig. 117—Pans of moist watercolors, used by professionals. These are easily diluted in water and offer an extraordinary quality and intensity of color. They come in palette boxes of 6, 12, 14 or 24 different colors, and refills for individual colors are available.

117

Fig. 118—Tubes of creamy watercolor also used by professionals. Their consistency is similar to that of oil paints. They have the advantage of dissolving immediately, with the same intensity and transparency as the moist watercolor tablets. They come in metal tubes in several sizes in palette boxes that generally hold 12 colors. Separate colors can also be obtained.

118

Fig. 119—Jars of liquid watercolor for professional use, especially for illustrators. These are similar to aniline pigments, with great strength and intensity, and are occasionally used in artistic watercolor painting for backgrounds or wide gradations of color. They come in boxes of 6 or 12 bottles, and refills are available.

119

Fig. 120—As mentioned previously, paint manufacturers package pans and tubes in metal boxes that also serve as palettes, but most professionals feel that the watercolor palette should be expressly made for that purpose. The two models shown in the illustration are like those most commonly used by watercolor artists, with slight variations.

watercolor color chart

As you can see, this color chart offers 81 colors plus China white. Another color chart, by Winsor & Newton, offers 86 different colors including 14 yellows, 9 reds, 11 blues, and 10 greens, you do not need such a variety of colors to paint, but in art as well as in school, each "teacher has his preferred text." I use three classic blues: cobalt blue, ultramarine, and Prussian blue. The color charts present a large variety of colors enabling artists to study, experiment, and finally choose their own spectrum of colors. As we will see on the following pages, this does not clash with the idea of a standard palette used by professional artists.

Please note that here, as in all other color ranges, two to five small crosses represent a greater or lesser degree of permanence, depending on the classification as temporary or permanent. We know that crimson, madder lakes, Prussian blue, olive green, and all yellows except cadmium yellow have a low rating on the permanence scale. This is based on how long they last when the watercolor painting is exposed to direct light for some time. Needless to say, no one exposes watercolors or oil paintings to intense light for a long time. If you visit the National Gallery in London, you will appreciate watercolors painted over 150 years ago that have not lost the luminosity of their colors. The manufacturer's warning about how permanent colors really are is to be taken into account, but one should not worry excessively about it.

One must take into account the fact that watercolors lose between 10 and 20% of their intense color between the time they are applied and the moment they dry. This color can be regained through the use of fixatives. We will discuss this later on.

214 ①★★★
Chromorange (bleifrei)
chrome orange
chrome orangé véritable
arancione di cromo
naranja cromo

215 ②★★★★
Echtgelb hell
permanent yellow light
jaune permanent clair
giallo permanente chiaro
amarillo permanente claro

216 ②★★★★
Echtgelb mittel
permanent yellow middle
jaune permanent moyen
giallo permanente medio
amarillo permanente medio

217 ②★★★★
Echtgelb dunkel
permanent yellow deep
jaune permanent foncé
giallo permanente scuro
amarillo permanente oscuro

218 ②★★★★
Echtorange
permanent orange
orangé permanent
arancione permanente
naranja permanente

220 ②★★★★
Indischgelb
indian yellow
jaune indien
giallo indiano
amarillo indio

221 ①★★★
Jaune brillant
brilliant yellow light
jaune brillant véritable
giallo brillante chiaro
amarillo brillante claro

223 ③★★★★
Kadmiumgelb zitron
cadmium yellow lemon
jaune cadmium citron
giallo di cadmio limone
amarillo cadmio limón

224 ③★★★★★
Kadmiumgelb hell
cadmium yellow light
jaune cadmium clair
giallo di cadmio chiaro
amarillo cadmio claro

225 ③★★★★★
Kadmiumgelb mittel
cadmium yellow middle
jaune cadmium moyen
giallo di cadmio medio
amarillo cadmio medio

226 ③★★★★★
Kadmiumgelb dunkel
cadmium yellow deep
jaune cadmium foncé
giallo di cadmio scuro
amarillo cadmio oscuro

227 ③★★★★★
Kadmiumorange hell
cadmium orange light
orangé cadmium clair
arancione di cadmio chiaro
naranja cadmio claro

228 ③★★★★★
Kadmiumorange dunkel
cadmium orange deep
orangé cadmium foncé
arancione di cadmio scuro
naranja cadmio oscuro

229 ①★★★★★
Neapelgelb
naples yellow
jaune de naples
giallo di napoli
amarillo nápoles

230 ①★★★★
Neapelgelb rötlich
naples yellow reddish
jaune de naples rougeâtre
giallo di napoli rossastro
amarillo nápoles rojizo

345 ②★
Echtrot tief
permanent red deep
rouge permanent foncé
rosso permanente scuro
rojo permanente oscuro

346 ②★
Echtrosa
permanent rose
rose permanent
rosa permanente
rosa permanente

348 ③★
Kadmiumrot hellst
cadmium red pale
rouge cadmium extra-clair ve
rosso di cadmio chiarissimo
rojo cadmio pálido

349 ③★
Kadmiumrot hell
cadmium red light
rouge cadmium clair véritabl
rosso di cadmio chiaro
rojo cadmio claro

350 ③★
Kadmiumrot dunkel
cadmium red deep
rouge cadmium foncé véritab
rosso di cadmio scuro
rojo cadmio oscuro

353 ②
Karmin
carmine
carmin
carminio
carmin

355
Karminrot
carmine red
rouge de carmin
rosso di carminio
rojo carmin

356
Krapplack hell
madder lake light
laque de garance claire
lacca di garanza chiara
laca garanza clara

358
Krapplack dunkel
madder lake deep
laque de garance foncé
lacca di garanza scura
laca garanza oscura

359 ②
Krapp-Karmin
madder carmine
carmin de garance
carminio di garanza
carmin de garanza

360 ②
Permanentrot 1
permanent red 1
rouge permanent 1
rosso permanente 1
rojo permanente 1

361 ②
Permanentrot 2
permanent red 2
rouge permanent 2
rosso permanente 2
rojo permanente 2

362 ②
Permanentrot 3
permanent red 3
rouge permanent 3
rosso permanente 3
rojo permanente 3

363 ②
Scharlachlack
scarlet lake
laque de garance écarlate
lacca scarlatta
laca escarlata

365 ①★★
Zinnoberrot
vermilion
vermillon
vermiglione
Bermellón

121

480
Bergblau ②★★★★
mountain blue
bleu de montagne
blu di montagna
azul montaña

481
Cölinblau ③★★★★
cerulean blue
bleu ceruleum véritable
blu celeste
azul celeste

483
Echtviolett ②★★★★
permanent violet
violet permanent
viola permanente
violeta permanente

484
Phthaloblau ②★★★★★
phthalo blue
bleu phthalo
blu phthalo
azul phthalo

485
Indigo ①★★★★
indigo
indigo
indaco
indigo

486
Kobaltblau imit. ①★★★★★
cobalt blue imit.
bleu de cobalt imit.
blu di cobalto imitazione
azul cobalto imit.

487
Kobaltblau hell ③★★★★★
cobalt blue light
bleu cobalt clair véritable
blu di cobalto chiaro
azul cobalto claro

488
Kobaltblau dunkel ③★★★★★
cobalt blue deep
bleu cobalt foncé véritable
blu di cobalto scuro
azul cobalto oscuro

489
Kobaltviolett dunkel ③★★★★★
cobalt violet deep
violet cobalt foncé véritable
viola di cobalto scuro
violeta cobalto oscuro

490
Magenta ①★★★
magenta
magenta
viola di magenta
magenta

491
Pariserblau ①★★★★
paris blue
bleu de paris
blu di parigi
azul paris

492
Preußischblau ①★★★★
prussian blue
bleu de prusse
blu di prussia
azul prusia

493
Purpurviolett ②★★
purple violet
violet pourpre
viola porpora
violeta púrpura

494
Ultramarin feinst ②★★★★★
ultramarine finest
outremer extra-fin
blu oltremare finissimo
ultramar fino

495
Ultramarinviolett ②★★★★★
ultramarine violet
violet outremer
viola oltremare
violeta ultramar

496
Ultramarinblau ①★★★★★
ultramarine blue
bleu outremer
blu oltremare
azul ultramar

497
Violett feurig ②★★
glowing violet
violet lumineux
viola luminoso
violeta luminoso

516
Grüne Erde ①★★★★★
green earth
terre vert
terra verde
tierra verde

517
Grünlack hell ②★★★★
green lake light
laque vert clair
lacca verde chiara
laca verde clara

518
Grünlack dunkel ②★★★★
green lake deep
laque vert foncé
lacca verde scura
laca verde oscura

519
Phthalogrün ②★★★★
phthalo green
vert de phthalo
verde phthalo
verde phthalo

520
Hookersgrün 1 ②★★★★
hooker's green 1
vert de hooker 1
verde di hooker 1
verde hooker 1

521
Hookersgrün 2 ②★★★★
hooker's green 2
vert de hooker 2
verde di hooker 2
verde hooker 2

522
Kobaltgrün hell ③★★★★★
cobalt green light
vert cobalt clair vérit.
verde di cobalto chiaro
verde cobalto claro

523
Kobaltgrün dunkel ③★★★★★
cobalt green deep
vert cobalt foncé vérit.
verde di cobalto scuro
verde cobalto oscuro

524
Maigrün ②★★★★
may green
vert de mai
verde primavera
verde primavera

525
Olivengrün ①★★★★
olive green
vert olive
verde oliva
verde oliva

526
Permanentgrün hell ①★★★★
permanent green light
vert permanent clair
verde permanente chiaro
verde permanente claro

527
Permanentgrün dunkel ②★★★★★
permanent green deep
vert permanent foncé
verde permanente scuro
verde permanente oscuro

528
Preußischgrün ①★★★★
prussian green
vert de prusse
verde di prussia
verde prusia

529
Saftgrün 1 ②★★★★
sap green 1
vert forêt 1
verde bosco 1
verde bosque 1

530
Saftgrün 2 ②★★★★
sap green 2
vert forêt 2
verde bosco 2
verde savia 2

531
Zinnobergrün hell ①★★★★
vermilion green light
vert cinabre clair
verde vermiglione chiaro
verde bermellón claro

532
Zinnobergrün dunkel ①★★★★
vermilion green deep
vert cinabre foncé
verde vermiglione scuro
verde cinabrio oscuro

650
Englischrot dunkel ①★★★★★
english red deep
rouge anglais foncé
rosso inglese scuro
rojo inglés oscuro

651
Goldocker ①★★★★★
golden ochre
ocre or
ocra oro
ocre dorado

653
Grüne Erde gebrannt ①★★★★★
burnt green earth
terre verte brûlée
terra verde bruciata
tierra verde tostada

655
Lichter Ocker 1 ①★★★★★
yellow ochre 1
ocre jaune 1
giallo ocra 1
ocre amarillo 1

656
Lichter Ocker 2 ①★★★★★
yellow ochre 2
ocre jaune 2
giallo ocra 2
ocre amarillo 2

657
Lichter Ocker gebrannt ①★★★★★
burnt yellow ochre
ocre jaune brûlée
giallo ocra bruciato
ocre ama. tostado

658
Madderbraun ②★★★
brown madder
laque de garance brun-rouge
lacca di garanza bruna
laca garanza marrón

660
Siena natur ①★★★★★
raw sienna
terre de sienne naturelle
terra di siena naturale
siena natural

661
Siena gebrannt ①★★★★★
burnt sienna
terre de sienne brûlée
terra di siena bruciata
siena tostada

662
Sepiabraun col. ①★★★★
sepia brown tone
teinte sepia
tinta di seppia bruciata
tinta sepia

663
Sepiabraun ①★★★★
sepia brown
brun sepia
seppia bruciata
sepia

664
Stil de grain brun ①★★★★★
brown pink
stil de grain brun
stil di grain bruno
stil grano marrón

665
Stil de grain vert ①★★★★★
green pink
stil de grain vert
stil di grain verde
stil grano verde

666
Terra Pozzuoli ①★★★★★
pozzuoli earth
terre de pouzzoles
terra di pozzuoli
tierra pozzuoli

667
Umbra natur ①★★★★★
raw umber
terre ombre naturelle verdâtre
terra d'ombra naturale
sombra natural

668
Umbra gebrannt ①★★★★★
burnt umber
terre d'ombre brûlée
terra d'ombra bruciata
sombra tostada

669
Vandyckbraun ①★★★★★
vandyke brown
brun van dyck
bruno van dyck
pardo van dyck

watercolors commonly used

Lemon yellow*

Cadmium yellow deep

Yellow ochre

Raw umber*

Sepia

Cadmium red

Alizarin crimson

Permanent green*

Emerald green

Cobalt blue*

Ultramarine

Prussian blue

Payne's gray

Ivory black*

The British masters of the 18th century, Cozens, Girtin, and even Turner, used a limited palette of only 5 or 6 colors. You do not really need more than that to depict what surrounds you in nature. Actually, all you need to make new colors is the appropriate mixture of red, yellow, and blue. However, let us be practical and see what other colors can enrich our palette.

While researching which colors are most frequently used, we found that most manufacturers sell watercolors in boxes of 17 tubes. The manufacturers answered our question and we are able to accept their choices because they know what sells. Their assortment of colors is not chosen haphazardly and most beginners start with this same range. With time, professionals determine their own palette, which will be adapted to their style and interpretation. Until you reach that point, allow me to explain a somewhat universal color assortment.

The basic colors which are found in all prepackaged assortments are cadmium yellow or cadmium yellow deep, yellow ochre, cadmium red, alizarin crimson, emerald green, ultramarine, and ivory black. You just have to add some blues and a gray like Payne's gray, which to me is an indispensable color. The following is a list of the most commonly used colors:

Fig. 122—Following a logical line of reasoning, we believe that this selection of colors represents those most commonly used by the professional artist. To limit the number even further, the colors indicated with an asterisk could also be eliminated: lemon yellow, raw umber, permanent green, cobalt blue, and ivory black.

WATERCOLORS COMMONLY USED	
Lemon yellow*	Permanent green*
Cadmium yellow deep	Emerald green
Yellow ochre	Cobalt blue*
Raw umber*	Ultramarine
Sepia	Prussian blue
Cadmium red	Payne's gray
Alizarin crimson	Ivory black*

tempera colors (gouache)

Gouache or tempera colors have a great similarity to watercolors and therefore merit a discussion in this book. Temperas are diluted with water and you need the same type of brushes and paper as you do with watercolors. The main difference between temperas and watercolors is that the former has a larger quantity of pigment or colored earth, the binding agent is glue, and the lighter tones are obtained by the admixture of white pigment.

Because of this difference we observe the following:

**Watercolors have a distinctive transparency.
Temperas are characterized
by their opaqueness.**

Temperas are opaque, thick, covering paints that allow you to use light colors over dark colors. If you dilute temperas with a lot of water, the resulting product is somewhat similar to watercolors. I would like to emphasize that the major characteristics of temperas are their opaqueness and their matte finish. They remind one of some oil paintings.

Fig. 123—Tempera paints or gouache are made up of the same ingredients as watercolor, but the pigments are bound with glue and the lighter tones are obtained by the admixture of white pigment. Tempera paints produce a matte, opaque finish, making it possible to paint light colors over dark. They are sold in metal tubes or small glass jars.

123

124

Fig. 124—Joseph Mallord William Turner *Petworth Interior*, sketch on gray paper, British Museum, London.

the palette box

Most of the metallic boxes that watercolors come in also double as a palette for mixing colors. These boxes are made of iron enameled in white. They have a series of concave divisions that are square or rectangular and allow you to mix the different colors separately. In some boxes you can separate the tray with the paints and this leaves you with a mixing palette of two or three trays. One of them even has a hole for your left thumb or a ring that allows you to hold the palette with your left hand while you mix colors with your right hand.

Professionals normally use palettes like the one shown on page 63. There are two styles, each suited to a different type of watercolor. This allows you to use the palette most appropriate to moist watercolors, tablets, or creamy tube watercolors. In case you do not have any palette a white china plate will do. Many artists also use an "auxiliary palette" which is a piece of white watercolor paper where they try out the desired effect before applying it to the painting.

As you know, all color charts and many of these palette boxes have a thick white, similar in texture to temperas, called China white. What is the reason for and use of this white? After all, the basic principle of using watercolor is to work with the paper's white. This question must remain unanswered. There may be some unorthodox artists who use it to create a certain play of light in profiles or reflections, or for the white of a ship's ropes or small white wildflowers. But it should not be used—it is like cheating! As you will see from your reading of this book there are other methods that can be used without breaking the rules of good watercolor painting.

Fig. 125—Miniature set with case, palette box, brush and a small jar for water (the closed case measures 9 × 11cm, 3.5" × 4.5"); it can be carried in a pocket with a small pad of paper to do notes while traveling, in the country, etc.

Fig. 126—Palette box with dry watercolor cakes of the grade called scholastic. Underneath the tray of colors there is a ring that can be used to support the box with the left thumb as if it were a palette.

125

126

Fig. 127—Large palette box with 24 pans of moist watercolors. The tray with the colors can be separated from the metal box, leaving more space to mix colors. In the center tray a rivet (A) can be seen which secures the ring for holding the palette with the left thumb. When the session is over, the tray with paints is replaced in the box and the set can be folded and closed.

Fig. 128—Palette box with 12 tubes of professional quality watercolor. The tubes can be taken out of the box and the box can be used as a palette. It has a hole through which the left thumb can be slipped to hold it.

127

128

moisteners, masking fluid, fixatives, and more

a   b   c   d   e   f   g   h

The only liquid that is absolutely necessary for working in watercolor is tap water. There are, however, a few liquids, such as moisteners and astringents, that improve the quality of the water you will be working with. There are also products such as masking fluid that allow you to achieve special effects. The following paragraphs describe these products and their characteristics.

Masking Fluid: This product is especially designed to set off the small areas that create a special brilliance, a twinkle, or a linear form such as a tree trunk or a thin branch. You apply it with a brush and allow it to dry. This creates a waterproof film which you can later remove with your finger or a regular eraser. To apply the masking fluid, use an old brush that can be cleaned with ethyl alcohol. Open spaces can also be set off prior to painting by using white wax.

Medium Number 2: This is a solution of acidified gum that should be added to your water with an eyedropper. It will eliminate all oily traces from the water and give the colors greater intensity, shine, and transparency.

Refined Oxgall: This is a moistening product that you mix with the water to increase the clinging power and flow of the colors. Pour a small amount of the refined oxgall into half a liter of water.

Glycerine: When you paint outdoors on a very sunny or windy day your watercolors will dry faster than expected. This problem can be avoided by adding some glycerine to your water. This method of prolonging the drying time should also be used when you need the painting to dry slowly.

96° Alcohol: Sometimes you will find that you need to speed up the drying process. This usually happens on wet, rainy days or if you are painting by the seashore. The solution to this problem is to add some alcohol (96 proof) to the water. It is known that 18th-century British artists added cognac or gin to their water instead of alcohol. This sort of makes you wonder as to what it is they actually did at Monto's school.

Varnish: Almost all manufacturers of watercolors also produce a special varnish. This product is used by some artists to protect and add brilliance to their paintings. Many professionals do not believe in using varnishes because watercolors should have a matte finish. I know that some artists add the varnish in layers and only in certain areas, particularly in dark colors so they will appear less intense and offer less contrast when they dry out. We do recommend that you do not use many layers of varnish to avoid giving the watercolor the shiny finish of a plastic-covered print.

Fig. 129—Here is a series of auxiliary products for watercolor painting. From left to right: a) masking fluid for setting off open spaces prior to painting; b) medium to prepare the water better; c) refined oxgall, as a moistening agent; d) glycerine to mix with the water and slow the drying of the paint; e) alcohol of 96 to mix with the water to speed drying; f, g, and h) varnish for the watercolor once it is completed. From a professional point of view, the masking fluid, medium, and watercolor varnish are the most essential.

water

There is no uniform criterion among artists on how many (one or two) or what type (glass or plastic) water jars should be used when painting outdoors or in the studio. Some artists use two jars, the first to loosen the paint and the second to wash the brush. Another school of thought believes that when you work with one jar you are "dirtying" the brush and this will ultimately help you by making your colors blend better. Artists who work outdoors like to use plastic jars for obvious reasons. They do not want to risk breaking a glass one. Personally, I am no lover of plastic and always use glass containers.

Regardless of the material you choose, the jar must hold between half a liter to a full liter (a pint to a quart) of water and have a wide mouth. Marmalade or mayonnaise jars fill all these requirements.

It is quite useful to have a blow dryer in your studio to quickly dry a specific area of your painting. How can you solve this problem outdoors where there are no electrical outlets? Many artists carry cigarette lighters with them and place the flame near the wet section to make it dry faster.

130

Fig. 130—Here are some suitable containers for the water: glass for the studio and plastic to carry along and avoid breakage. In either case, the container should hold at least a liter (quart) of water and it should have a wide mouth.

131

Fig. 131—The liquids on the preceding page, auxiliaries to watercolor painting, must be mixed with water with the exception of the masking fluid, which is applied directly to the watercolor with a brush. For mixing with water, it is a good idea to have an eyedropper on hand and to establish for yourself the exact quantities needed.

132

Fig. 132—When working in the studio, a method commonly used by professionals to speed the drying of the watercolors while working is to use an electric hairdryer on the wet area.

brushes for watercolor painting

The brushes used for painting watercolors have a wooden handle covered with shellac to which a metal band is attached. This band serves to hold the brush itself in place. Brush quality is determined by the animal hair used. The following types are available:

Sable hair brushes

Mongoose hair brushes

Ox hair brushes

Japanese deer hair brushes

Synthetic brushes

The best brush available is made with sable hair. The hair comes from the tails of Kolinski sables that live in Russia and China. The high price of these brushes is due to the fact that it is very difficult to make them. In order to lower the price, some manufacturers sell a brush made from a mixture of red sable and ox hair (which comes from the ox's ears). One step down in quality we have mongoose, squirrel, or ox hair brushes. The Japanese round brushes are excellent for painting oriental style watercolors called Sumie, but they are no better than other brushes. There is another Japanese brush, fan-shaped and perfect for painting rays of sunlight and wide graduated washes, that is very inexpensive. In the last few years there have been many synthetic brushes. These are quite inexpensive and well shaped, but cannot compare with the qualities found in sable hair brushes. The sable brush has sponge-like characteristics; it can absorb water and color, bend to the slightest manual pressure and yet maintain its perfect point.

Watercolor brushes come in different widths and are numbered from 00 to 1 to 2 ... up to 14 for sable hair brushes and 24 for ox hair brushes. These numbers are usually printed on the brush handle. The handle with the metal band measures about 20 cm in length.

To paint in watercolor, you need three sable hair brushes in sizes 8, 12, and 14 and a size 24 ox hair brush. We also recommend the use of a wide Japanese brush, a synthetic round sponge and a small natural sponge.

Fig. 133—This is the minimum assortment of brushes needed for watercolor painting; 3 sable brushes, nos. 8, 12, and 14, and an oxhair brush, no. 24.

133

Fig. 134—Here are some additional brushes to complement those in the preceding figure: a Japanese-style hake brush, a sponge in the shape of a roller, and a small natural sponge. These three items are necessary for resolving backgrounds and gradated washes. The sponge, which by the way must be natural and not synthetic, is also used to blot water or, occasionally, to paint.

134

Fig. 135—This picture shows a complete assortment of sable brushes, from numbers 00 to 10, plus 12 and 14.

Fig. 136—Other kinds of brushes available besides sable include the following, from left to right: 1 and 2: Wash brushes, typically French, of squirrel's hair, suitable for backgrounds and gradations. 3 and 4: Japanese brushes with bamboo handles and deer's hair. 5 and 6: Round synthetic fiber brushes for students. 7: Mongoose hair brush, stiffer than sable. 8: Special sable brush for drawing fine lines. 9: Fan-shaped boar's hair brush for rubbing and scraping. 10 and 11: Ox hair brushes used by many professionals, especially the higher-numbered ones.

135

136

brushes: their use and care

In watercolor as in oil painting, there are two ways of holding the brush. The first is just like a pencil only higher up and the second is with the handle in your fingertips as can be seen in figs. 137, 138, and 139. In both cases the distance is greater than the one normally used with a pencil, but it allows you to move the brush more freely, lengthens the arm, and lets you look at the painting from afar.

We have already said that brushes are expensive but with proper care a sable hair brush can last for years. The following rules should be carefully observed:

Never allow your brushes to stay in water for hours.

When you are done using them wash your brushes carefully, with soap and water if necessary.

Rinse them well and drain out the excess water.

Then with your fingertips, or better still between pursed lips, shape the point and allow it to dry in a jar with the hairs facing up.

When you are painting outdoors do not carry your brushes in your pocket or throw them in a box with other materials, a procedure which would be fatal to the hairs of the brush. Carefully roll the brushes in some cardboard or other stiff paper that will keep its shape, so that the brushes are immobile and the hairs protected from damage.

Figs. 137, 138, 139—These illustrations show the proper way to hold the brush while painting watercolors. Figs. 137 and 138 show the most common way, similar to the way one holds a pencil but farther from the brush end to make hand movements easier and to view the painting from a bit more distance so as to widen the angle of vision and appreciate the progress of the work as a whole better. Note in fig. 139, another way to hold the brush is with the handle in the fingertips, facilitating drawing and painting vertical or diagonal lines. This way, characteristic of the art of drawing or painting with pencil, charcoal, pastel, wax, etc., increases the artist's manual dexterity and technical ability.

138

137

139

Fig. 140—This photo shows how professional artist Guillermo Fresquet holds the handle almost perpendicular to the paper's surface.

140

other materials

141

Fig. 141—In addition to basic materials such as paints, brushes, and paper, the watercolor artist uses a series of auxiliary tools that are shown in this picture. Their description and uses follow. 1: A regular no. 2 lead pencil for watercolor drawing, or a higher quality HB pencil. 2: Normal white eraser of soft plastic and one of dark gray plastic, or one of similar quality to clean with. 3: Metal ruler 50 to 70 cm (20" to 30"). With a metal ruler, any type of blade can be used for cutting without danger of ruining the ruler. 4: T-square (not shown) and triangles. 5: Roll of gummed tape, 2 or 3 cm (1" or 11/2") wide for mounting and stretching the paper as explained in fig. 110 to 113. 6: Roll of adhesive tape, used to frame the painting before beginning to work. The tape is positioned like a frame, and comes off easily when finished, leaving the edges perfectly clean and sharp. 7: Thumbtacks and pins to hold down and stretch the paper when it is thick, thus avoiding the laborious traditional mounting and stretching with damp paper, gummed tape, etc. 8: A stick of white wax to set off areas to be left blank before painting, as will be explained later in the text. 9: Tissues to blot the brush before and after rinsing and to absorb moisture, water, or gouache in small or large areas. 10: Roll of paper towels, for the same use as the tissues, especially for blotting or squeezing out the brush when it is full of water or paint. 11: Plastic dish and moistened synthetic sponge to remove some of the color or moisture from the brush by holding it against the sponge. 12: Brush with a special beveled plastic handle to scratch and draw or to make light-colored, open spaces while the painted area is still moist (this type of brush is imported from Japan). 13: Cotton swabs for use in freshly painted areas, while still damp, to dry and absorb paint, leaving light-colored areas. 14: Razor blade to scratch and open spaces when the watercolor has dried. 15: Holder and nibs for drawing with India ink. The following items should also be mentioned: reed, black ballpoint, and black or gray finepoint marker, used interchangeably by the professional artist on occasion to draw lines or emphasize forms during the final stages or finishing touches of a watercolor. 16: India ink in stick form (it may also be liquid, in a normal jar) for drawing with the pen or reed. 17: Utility knife for cutting paper with the aid of the metal ruler. 18: Large scissors for cutting paper. 19: Container of rubber cement or special glue to glue paper to cardboard or wood before or after painting.

other materials

Watercolor painting demands a great many materials and tools that the artist must carry with him whenever he paints outdoors. It therefore becomes important to have a box, case, or bag where one will be able to carry colors, brushes, palette, sponge, paper towels, jars, liquids, and a long list of other things.

In view of this need many manufacturers produce elegant cases with basic materials, but which, despite their high prices, do not entirely solve the problem.

The solution would be a box or case for oil painting which you can adapt for using with watercolor, or an easel with a case incorporated such as the one seen in fig. 101, or the special one in fig. 142, reproduced here through the courtesy of Ceferino Olivé, a professional watercolor artist.

Fig. 142—Beautiful case of varnished hardwood, with metal catches and decorations, for carrying paints, brushes, ceramic palettes, and other materials and tools when painting out-of-doors.

Fig. 143—Typical case for oil paints, adapted for carrying watercolor materials and tools.

Fig. 144—This is a box designed by the professional watercolorist Ceferino Olivé. It measures approximately 75 × 52 cm (30" × 21"), making it possible to carry watercolor paper, a piece of plywood, a folding easel with tripod, and a plastic water jar, in addition to paints, palette, brushes, sponge, etc.

142

143

144

PLYWOOD

SHEET OF PAPER

PALETTE FOR WATERCOLORS

PLASTIC WATER JAR

JAR FOR WATER

SPONGE

CASE (72 × 52 cm)

TRAY FOR WATERCOLORS & BRUSH

FOLDING STOOL

FOLDING EASEL WITH TRIPOD

drawing:
the foundation
of watercolor

cube, cylinder, sphere

Peter Paul Rubens, aside from painting close to a thousand beautiful paintings, and producing thousands of drawings and sketches, also wrote a book. The book was titled: *Treatise of the Human Figure,* and in it, Rubens dictated a definitive norm in the art of drawing. Rubens said:

"The basic structure of the human figure may be reduced to the cube, the circle, and the triangle."

Almost 250 years later, Paul Cézanne reiterated Rubens' idea, amplifying it to include all subjects in nature. He told it to Monet, to Pissarro, to Vuillard, to Picasso, to everyone; in April 1904, he put it in writing in a letter to his friend Emile Bernard the painter. Cézanne told him:

"Everything in Nature is modeled after three fundamental shapes: the cube, the cylinder, and the sphere. It is necessary to learn how to draw these simple figures so that afterwards one will be able to do whatever one wants."

This is right, it's true.
If you are able to draw a cube (or rectangular prism), a cylinder, and a sphere perfectly well, you will be able to draw everything you are capable of seeing: the table, the chair, the glass,

your hand, your face, a figure, a landscape, everything. Because these and all forms may be fitted into and structured upon these "simple figures."

May I request that you draw these basic figures. In doing so, you will be practicing all the problems in the art of drawing, namely: the perspective of the forms, the problems of dimensions and proportions, chiaroscuro (the effects of light and shadow). After having finished this study, try to draw perceived or imaginary shapes starting out from the cube, the cylinder, and the sphere. I have done it here as if I were just beginning, remembering Rubens, and Cézanne. I can assure you that, being so simple, the experience is magnificent.

Fig. 146—As Cézanne said, "all the forms of all objects can be reduced to cubes, cylinders, and spheres." To draw these basic forms with a lead pencil or charcoal is, wihout a doubt, an extremely worthwhile exercise.

146

147

Fig. 147—The cube or rectangular prism helps indicate a linear or oblique perspective, the rules of which we will review in the following pages. For the moment, let us review how to draw a cube from an oblique perspective.

A

A. First draw the vertical line representing the edge nearest you.

B. From the end of this line, draw a slanted line representing the horizontal plane nearest you.

C

B

C. Next, draw the lateral plane "B."

D. Draw the top plane "C."

E. Finally, draw these lines as if the cube were made of glass, to check that the whole cube is drawn well.

Fig. 148—All objects can be constructed or "fitted" with a simple square, rectangle, circle and triangle. In most, if not all, cases this initial structure or fit can basically be formed with a cube, a rectangular prism, a cylinder, or a sphere. This has the advantage of putting the subject in perspective right from the start of drawing, and at the same time giving it the third dimension: volume.

148

fit, dimension, proportions

John Singer Sargent, the virtuoso American portrait painter, renowned for his extraordinary watercolors, told the following basic principle repeatedly to his students at the Royal Academy:

*"You must always cultivate
the power of observation."*

This is the key to constructing: the ability to calculate dimensions and proportions in order to draw. In a word: calculate, observe, compare, resolve. Let us take the example of the two roses and small pitcher drawn on the following page. With the aid of a pencil, the handle of a brush or a ruler, we first calculate the total height and width of the model (fig. 149). Realizing that, in this case, the height and width are practically the same, we draw a square, into

149

which we may "fit" the model (fig. 150). Now we compare some basic dimensions: the height of the small pitcher in relation to the total height of the model (A-A); the width of the flower on the upper right corner compared to the total width (B-b-B) of the picture. We try next to reduce and condense the *box* of the model. Assisted by the above calculations, we find a shape which conforms to these calculations (fig. 151). Next we imagine vertical and horizontal outlines which locate the shapes, distances, and proportions within the larger form (fig. 152). And at the same time, we study the spatial shapes of the empty spaces as in A, B, and C of fig. 153. Thus, we have taken on the problem, as Sargent described it, observing the model, calculating, and comparing.

150

Fig. 149—The model's basic structure or "fit" is determined by measuring and comparing its height with its width. These measurements are taken facing the model, arm extended, holding a pencil or brush handle in your hand. First the pencil is held vertically, to measure the height, then horizontally to measure width. Finally the relationship between the two measurements is calculated —for example, they may both be the same, or one may be double the other.

Fig. 150—Measuring the subject with a pencil or brush makes it possible to find its proportions, facilitating its "fit."

Fig. 151—Here, I can draw a more definite structure or fit within the rectangular box.

Fig. 152—In this or any model, vertical or horizontal lines can be imagined that pass through basic or reference points and allow you to situate and proportion forms, filling out the drawing.

Fig. 153—Another aid for estimating sizes and proportions is to try to imagine solid shapes in the open spaces (A, B, C). These are like molds that allow you to situate and define the actual shapes of your subject.

151

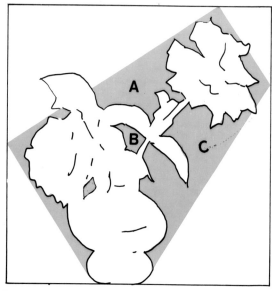

Fig. 154—It is certainly not easy to reduce the shape of a model like this one to the form of a cube, but in this as in all cases the drawing can be started with an overall box, square or rectangular, measured beforehand with a pencil or brush as explained in fig. 149. This basic form is then further broken down into smaller boxes inside the first one, with imaginary reference lines and points, and by trying to "see" shapes corresponding to the empty spaces, as explained in fig. 150 to 153 above. Studying the composition, dimensions, and proportions of examples like this one is a good exercise to keep your ability to draw and paint with watercolors sharp at all times.

154

light and shade: tonal values

Camille Corot, the artist and teacher, instructed Pissarro: "You are an artist, you don't need any advice save this: You must study value above all."

Values are tones; different tonalities are promoted by the effects of light and shade. Thanks to variation in values, we may represent the third dimension, that is the volume of forms, in drawing. One has to know the effects of light and shade—clarity, brilliance, shadow, projected shadow, chiaroscuro, and reflected light (fig. 155)—in order to evaluate tone. And one has to observe and compare carefully and constantly, in order to achieve a perfect evaluation.

To evaluate is to compare.

To evaluate is to mentally classify the tonalities and hues of a form, constantly comparing in order to determine which tones are more obscure, which most clear and which are the intermediate tones.

On this theme there is a practice procedure you may carry out right now: build yourself a cylinder out of thick white cardboard or Bristol board and draw your own left hand holding the cylinder, as I have done here, myself. Study the effects of the light and shadow, evaluate how the tones model the forms.

Fig. 155—Look at this drawing of a hand, my hand, as a study of the effects of light and shade and of tonal values, and note that the values are resolved with a limited spectrum of tones and that the volume of the objects depends on the following effects:

A. LIGHT: illuminated areas where the color is the model's own "local" color.

B. BRILLIANCE: obtained through contrast. Remember that "a white is whiter the darker the tone surrounding it is."

C. ACCENT: darkest part of the projected shadow, between the penumbra or cast shadow and the reflected light.

D. REFLECTED LIGHT: on the extreme edges of the shaded part. It is accented when there is a light-colored object next to the subject.

E. CHIAROSCURO: intermediate zone between the illuminated area and the area in shadow. The term *chiaroscuro* can be defined as light in shade

F. CAST SHADOW: the whole shaded area opposite the illuminated section.

G. PROJECTED SHADOW: the shadow that appears on the surface that the body is resting on (I have not drawn it here).

155

156

Fig. 156—To draw this hand, your hand, situate the cylinder in a vertical position and then try to find similar distances, such as A-A, and reference points and lines that allow you to estimate and resolve the subject's proportions and dimensions.

doing a quick sketch

Here is a practical exercise, especially designed for the watercolor painter, the resolution of which demands—from my point of view—remarkable technical understanding and drawing ability.

I would like you to draw rapidly, without previous preparation, without outlines, boxes or other structures, using a permanent medium such as ink which doesn't allow you to go back and rework or erase. A fine point marker or a black pen would be fine. Draw one or several objects seen from different angles—one of your hands, for instance— and resolve the drawing linearly, without lights or shadows, using only a minimum of lines to represent the basic shapes and the most important details of the model. I know that it's not easy, but I believe that it is useful and applicable if you keep in mind the reasons I will explain to you on the following page.

Fig. 157—Your left hand may be the best model for this freehand sketch. Try it; it is an excellent exercise for people like yourself who want to learn to paint in watercolor.

157

a special exercise

I assume that you are at home, sitting at your work table, or in your reading armchair, perhaps in your study. At any rate, may I ask you to look up in front of you and consider the possibility of drawing whatever you see before you. It may be necessary for you to go to another room in the house which offers more interesting drawing possibilities. At any rate, once you have found a setting which motivates you, draw it in a linear manner, eliminating light and shadow, and using a black pen.

I created this exercise at my work table in order to practice and explain how a drawing should be done from which you will paint a watercolor. Such a drawing should, first of all, be accurate and detailed, so that later, while painting, you will not get lost. When painting,

159

158

it should no longer be necessary to construct, so you may give all your attention to achieving hues, tonalities, and colors, that can make the watercolor into a masterpiece.

In the second place, the foundation drawing of a watercolor should be linear, without shadows or tones. But why? Well, because the interplay of lights and shadows should be explained with colors, not with the pencil. And this is due—let's not forget this—to the fact that watercolor is transparent. It is not difficult to imagine what would happen if we were to draw the shadows of this exercise in blacks and grays using a lead pencil and then paint on top of them. All the colors would be negatively affected, acquiring a gray and dirty tendency. (Unless one wishes to achieve this effect.) It should be pointed out that this exercise is simplified for practice purposes, but in actual practice, a drawing for a watercolor should be done with a lead or graphite pencil, HB or B, in order to make a less intense outline.

the right perspective

The themes of the watercolorist are often centered around streets and plazas, buildings, suburbs, and sea ports, places in which the perspective plays an important role. The great English masters of the watercolor were experts in perspective. But after all, we are artists, not architects, and we are capable of viewing and capturing the perspective by means of mastering only the basic rules which may be summarized as follows:

As you know, there are three kinds or classes of perspective:

1. *Parallel or vanishing point perspective.*
2. *Oblique perspective or perspective with two vanishing points.*
3. *Aerial perspective or perspective with three vanishing points.*

(This last kind is practically not used in artistic painting and will not be commented on here.)

The *vanishing point* is the place where the lines or perpendicular intersections of the model meet. These vanishing points are always located on the *horizon line,* which is just at the height of the viewer's eye, whether standing, sitting, or bending.

In the parallel perspective the single vanishing point and the viewpoint coincide in the same spot on the horizon. In oblique and aerial perspective, the vanishing points and the viewpoint are independent, although they still meet in the same horizon line.

Figs. 160, 161—Effects of linear perspective, with a single vanishing point that coincides with the viewpoint, applied to both cubes and to the inside of a tavern (left) and to the view of a street in an old neighborhood.

160

Figs. 162, 163—Two examples of side perspective with two vanishing points and a conventional viewpoint, applied to two cubes, an urban landscape (left), and a classic room interior.

162

Figures 160 and 161 show two examples of parallel one-point perspective. The first is applied to an interior, while the second looks at a typical street in an old neighborhood. In fig. 162 and 163, you may find two applications of oblique perspective.

Painting in watercolors such themes as the ones mentioned above, one often runs up against the problem of accurately dividing spaces or shapes that are repeated, such as the doors and windows of a house, a line of trees on a highway, or the arches of a cloister. For an expert painter, a problem of this kind doesn't represent any major difficulty. It is solved simply, calculating by sight. But I think it's good to know that there are a series of mathematical formulations that you can use. For example, you are painting the bars of an iron gate which from the front represent a symmetrical configuration. But to draw the gate in perspective, one has to calculate the per-

spective center. Figures 164 and 165 show the solution to this problem: an X-shaped cross with a vertical line down its center was drawn (fig. 165) in order to obtain the perspective center.

In figs. 166 and 167 you will find a really easy solution for solving the problem of dividing receding spaces which have repeated shapes, in this case, the romantic cloister of an old church.

166

Figs. 164, 165—To put in perspective the center of a model that, seen from the front, is symmetrical (fig. 162) you just need to draw the figure's square or rectangle in perspective and then find its perspective center by drawing an X.

Fig. 166—(Right). These pictures show how to divide spaces in depth and perspective.

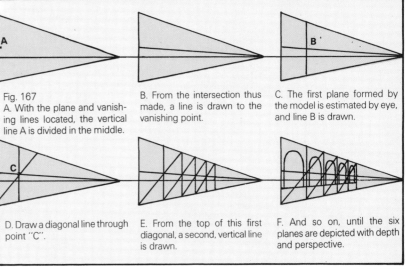

Fig. 167
A. With the plane and vanishing lines located, the vertical line A is divided in the middle.

B. From the intersection thus made, a line is drawn to the vanishing point.

C. The first plane formed by the model is estimated by eye, and line B is drawn.

D. Draw a diagonal line through point "C".

E. From the top of this first diagonal, a second, vertical line is drawn.

F. And so on, until the six planes are depicted with depth and perspective.

167

the right perspective

168

In the drawing in fig. 168, two typical problems of the division of receding spaces are illustrated: a wall with a *determined* number of equal spaces within a space which is also determined, and a mosaic; both in parallel perspective, seen from a single viewpoint. Note in fig 168 schemes A and B, the solution to the first problem is found by tracing a *ground line* and then dividing it into equal spaces (169 A). Diagonal lines were then drawn to vanishing point E, thus determining the depth of the calculated spaces. In regard to the mosaic in parallel perspective (fig. 170, A, B, and C), it is only necessary to calculate by sight the dimension of rectangle a-b and use it as a base. We then make a series of diagonals to the vanishing point, tracing the quadrille ruling of scheme C, which allows us to draw the mosaic in perspective.

170 A

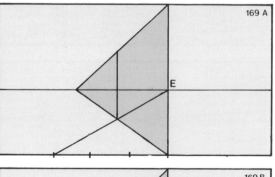

169 A

Figs. 168, 169—Here is the formula (A and B) for putting a defined number of equal planes into perspective within another defined plane, in this case, the right side wall in the interior of the regal salon in fig. 168.

Fig. 170—In sketches A, B, and C of this figure, you can see the way to draw a mosaic in linear perspective, from a single point, using a grid drawn in perspective.

170 B

169 B

170 C

1. How to find the center of a square in oblique perspective.
2. How to divide the depth of a given space into equal parts in oblique perspective (figs. 170 A and B).
3. How to draw a mosaic or grid in oblique perspective (figs. 171 A-F).

Let me suggest that you try these perspective exercises on a larger scale than the figures here, at least double their size.

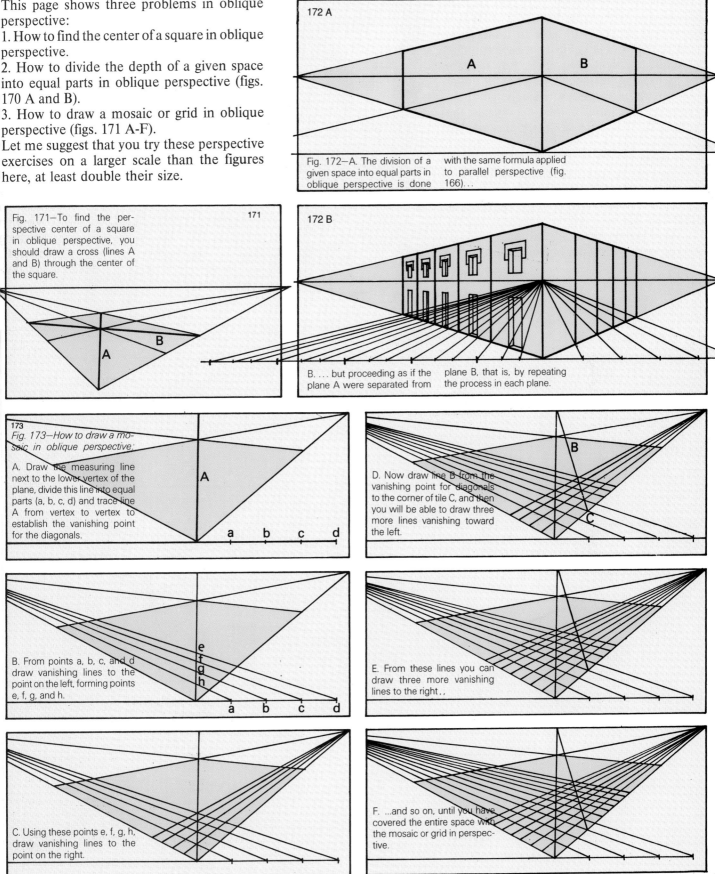

172 A

Fig. 172—A. The division of a given space into equal parts in oblique perspective is done with the same formula applied to parallel perspective (fig. 166)...

Fig. 171—To find the perspective center of a square in oblique perspective, you should draw a cross (lines A and B) through the center of the square.

171

172 B

B. ... but proceeding as if the plane A were separated from plane B, that is, by repeating the process in each plane.

173

Fig. 173—How to draw a mosaic in oblique perspective:

A. Draw the measuring line next to the lower vertex of the plane, divide this line into equal parts (a, b, c, d) and trace line A from vertex to vertex to establish the vanishing point for the diagonals.

D. Now draw line B from the vanishing point for diagonals to the corner of tile C, and then you will be able to draw three more lines vanishing toward the left.

B. From points a, b, c, and d draw vanishing lines to the point on the left, forming points e, f, g, and h.

E. From these lines you can draw three more vanishing lines to the right, ,

C. Using these points e, f, g, h, draw vanishing lines to the point on the right.

F. ...and so on, until you have covered the entire space with the mosaic or grid in perspective.

the right perspective

If you have studied and practiced the exercises in perspective explained on the preceding pages, you will now be able to understand easily the last and possibly the most important technique of artistic perspective. It is to establish by eye the perspective offered by buildings, streets, and plazas. Usually, in these cases, the vanishing points are outside the painting or the space in which the artist is drawing or painting. How do you make the windows, doors, rooftops and ledges of a street or plaza like the one I have drawn in fig. 174 appear in perfect perspective? Note the solution in sketches 175 A, B, and C, and keep in mind that this is a simple, practical technique for drawing freehand, without rulers or squares, with the model in front of you.

174

175

Fig. 174—Drawing or painting subjects like this, the perspective must be judged by eye, but there is a simple technique that can be applied that essentially solves all the difficulties.

Fig. 175—A. The model is framed loosely, establishing with extreme care the angle of the basic lines that vanish to the horizon.
Then the vertical "A" is drawn, corresponding to the highest corner, and this line is divided into a specified number of equal parts, six in this example.

B. Now we will step out of the painting; at the paper's left margin, we draw another vertical and we divide it also into six equal sections.

C. Finally, we draw a new vertical, also outside the drawing, in the right margin, divide it into six equal parts, and join points A with A, B with B, etc., forming a guide-pattern that enables us to draw all the model's parts in perfect perspective. The whole set of lines and measures for this technique, the verticals, their division into equal parts, and the sketching of a guide-pattern in perspective, must be done by eye and freehand, without a ruler or T-square. It is truly a technique for artists.

aerial perspective, atmosphere, contrast

In addition to linear perspective, the artist should keep *atmosphere*, or aerial perspective, in mind. The author of *The System of the Arts*, Hegel, says in this regard that all objects in the real world show a variation in color due to the atmosphere that surrounds them. The intensity of the colors is diluted with distance—this is what is meant by aerial perspective. Leonardo da Vinci, in his *Treatise on Painting*, followed a similar line of reasoning:

"The foreground should be finished in a clear and precise manner; the middle ground should be equally complete, but in a more vaporous way, more diffuse; and so on, depending on the distance, the contours should be softer, and forms and colors should disappear little by little."

In a landscape with mountains in the background it is easy to verify this phenomenon of intervening atmosphere, noting that the nearest mountains offer more intense color than those farther away, and also noting that in the foreground there is more contrast of tone and color and better definition than in the background. We could say, in summarizing these effects, that:

Contrast and definition decrease with intervening atmosphere.

As you know, when painting in watercolor, these effects of contrast and definition are obtained, by diluting the outlines in the background with water, that is, by painting, "wet," while the foreground is preferably done "dry." Furthermore, contrast is increased by highlighting the light-colored areas of the foreground with dark tones, recalling the classic rules of *simultaneous contrasts*:

The darker the tone surrounding it, the lighter a white or light color appears to be.

Contrast can also be achieved by juxtaposing complementary colors, but we will leave this technique for later pages.

Fig. 176—In the city, on the sea, in the countryside, the intervening atmosphere softens the contrast and definition of the background, which offer less color and appear grayer the farther away from the viewer they are.

Fig. 177—The foreground is the darkest area and at the same time the clearest, that is to say, the foreground displays greater contrast and therefore greater definition. As we will see in the sketch, the farther away the planes are the grayer they are and the more contrast they lose. When these techniques are kept in mind, the painting achieves greater depth.

176

177

Fig. 178—The darker the tone surrounding it, the whiter a white appears. This law, called the law of *simultaneous contrasts*, can be appreciated in this example. The shine of ceramic B seems whiter than that of ceramic A because the tone surrounding B is darker.

A

B

178

plato's rule

To compose a watercolor painting... Yes, but first we should ask what is composition and, above all, how is a watercolor painting composed? To the first question—what is composition?—many artists and art experts have responded. Matisse, for example, the famous painter, wrote this fine definition: "Composition is the art of arranging the various elements that the artist has at his disposal for expressing his feelings in a decorative fashion." And Peter and Linda Murray, authors of the *Dictionary of Art and Artists*, published by Penguin, also define the term *composition* perfectly, saying that "it is the operation of combining the elements of a picture to achieve a satisfactory visual whole." Fine, but HOW are these elements (which elements?) of the painting *arranged* or *combined* to express the artist's feelings and, at the same time, "to achieve a satisfactory whole"? There is no concrete answer to this question, only rules like those of Plato or Vitruvius that give us some guidance.

Plato, as you know, was one of the great philosophers of ancient Greece, who taught his students as he strolled with them, as was the custom at that time. One of his students asked him one day how to compose a painting. Plato simply responded:

"Find and represent the variety within the unity."

That is, find variety in the form, in the color, in the situation, in the size and arrangement of the elements that make up the painting, so that this variety attracts the attention and awakens the interest of the viewer, inducing him to look and finally, giving him the pleasure of looking and contemplating. But be careful; when this variety is so great that it becomes disconcerting and disperses the attention initially attracted, the viewer tires and the painting ceases to interest him. The variety must be organized in some order and within a unity of the whole, combining the two ideas to establish:

UNITY within variety

VARIETY within unity

See the adjoining sketches and texts for an explanation of Plato's rule through pictures.

179

180

Fig. 179—*Excessive Unity*. Color and form offer few variants; the arrangement of the elements is static, symmetrical; the whole model displays too much uniformity, a lack of variety that can be monotonous and uninteresting for the viewer looking at the painting.

Fig. 180—*Excessive Variety*. Here, on the other hand, an attempt has been made to diversify, varying forms, colors, arrangement, and so on to such an extreme that the necessary unity has been lost, creating a dispersed composition that may cause the viewer to tire and lose interest.

181

Fig. 181—*Variety within Unity*. The painting's elements now offer variety in form, color and arrangement, and at the same time, there is an order to these elements, a unity that creates a satisfactory visual whole.

vitruvius' golden section

In the days of the Roman Emperor Augustus, an architect named Vitruvius studied the organization of forms and space from an aesthetic point of view. Vitruvius wondered even then what the perfect arrangement, artistically speaking, of a point or dividing line within a give space might be.

But let me explain Vitruvius' proposition to you with some drawings:

Imagine a given area—the painting—in which we are to place the principal figure of the picture. If we place this figure in the center, we will obtain a symmetrical composition, appropriate for certain themes (solemn, majestic, religious, etc.) but without the variety necessary for modern composition. If we move this figure to one edge of the painting, the variety may become exaggerated. This is when the question arises as to where to place the figure. Vitruvius finally resolved this problem by establishing the famous *Golden Section* or *Golden rule:*

"For an area divided into unequal sections to be agreeable and aesthetic, there should be the same relationship between the larger section and the whole as between the smaller and larger sections."

The Law of the Golden Section

Let us imagine a segment whose total length is 5 cm.

2 cm.   3 cm.

If we divide this area into two sections of 2 cm, we will see that, according to Vitruvius' law, the same proportional relationship exists between the smaller portion (2 cm) and the larger one (3 cm) as between the larger section (3 cm) and the whole, or the entire length (5 cm). This is so because 5:3=3:20 If you reduce these simple fractions you will obtain the same results—1:6. Vitruvius thus found this numerical relationship in "extreme and mean ratio," establishing that:

The arithmetical expression of the "Golden Section" is equal to 1.618

Practically speaking, when you want to find the division of a Golden Section, multiply the total length of the space by the factor 0.618. Look at the following examples:

185

186

GOLDEN POINT

Figs. 185, 186—The law of the Golden Section can be applied both to the height and the width of the painting. Where both sections cross, they form the golden point, considered the ideal place to situate the painting's principal figure. By means of a simple change in the division of the segments, the golden point can be located in four different places.

182

183

Fig. 182—Dividing the painting in the center and placing its principal element right in the middle, we end up with a symmetrical composition, monotonous because of its lack of variation.

Fig. 183—Moving the painting's principal element to one side, the composition is asymmetrical, but it may present an excessive variation, detracting from the painting's aesthetic quality.

Fig. 184—Applying the law of the Golden Section to the height and width of the painting, we obtain a *golden point* that lets us situate the painting's principal figure in just the right place. Furthermore, this improves the placement of the level that limits the background (A), which we now situate at exactly the height of the Golden Section.

184

A

compositional schemes

Here is another device that you can use to compose a painting: *the device of geometric schemes.*

Scientifically proven, simple, and eminently practical, this technique was established in practice by the German philosopher Fechner, who was the first to study the relationship between the physical and psychic effects of form. Fechner succeeded in proving, with surveys and statistics, that most people, when asked to choose between a series of geometric shapes, a series of natural shapes, and another series of abstract forms, prefer geometric shapes because of their simple, concrete configuration. C. P. Haas, expert in images, offers the opinion that this truly bewitching power of geometric forms is a consequence of the principle of hedonism. "Obtain the most satisfaction with the least effort," or the principle of muscular, nervous, or mental economy...

Let us hasten to explain, however, that geometric forms had already been in use in artistic composition for hundreds of years, first with the adoption of the triangle (A), a perfect scheme of symmetric composition, and afterwards with the *diagonal scheme*, suggested and

applied principally by Rembrandt, and associated with asymmetrical composition.

Well then, when it is time to choose the subject and determine how to frame it, try to find an overall form that corresponds to a particular geometric shape. And be sure that your watercolor will offer "a satisfactory visual whole."

This page shows some examples of geometric shapes and their application to watercolor painting.

187

188

Figs. 187 to 191—Here are some watercolors that show some of the geometric shapes presented on this page.

the third dimension

Representing the third dimension, or what amounts to the same thing—highlighting the effect of depth by showing the space intervening between one point and another—is also an important factor in the art of composing a painting.

Here, then, are the techniques that the artist can use to emphasize depth:

A) Including in the painting a well-defined foreground. By painting a group of trees, a fence, or any other object of known dimensions and size in the foreground with the middle ground and beyond, mentally establishing in a mechanical way the distance between one plane and another, and as a result the painting's depth.

B) Superimposing successive planes: When the foreground of a landscape shows some trees or bushes, some rocks, or a fence, and includes in the middle ground beyond, say, the houses of a small town crowded together, and beyond that or in the background a taller building, a church or small mountain, we have a subject composed of *successive superimposed planes*, perfectly defined by Plato's formula of "variety within unity," allowing us to represent and highlight the third dimension depth.

C) Painting in perspective: The third dimension is represented in drawings done in perspective: streets, squares, buildings, roads, rows of trees, etc. But the viewpoint, the framing that allows us to dramatize the effect of depth, must be chosen with forethought.

D) Highlighting the contrast and atmosphere: These concepts are directly related to the different planes of the painting, to the impression of space and depth. It is a matter of remembering this technique and accentuating it when in front of your subject.

E) Painting "near" and "far" colors. It has been shown that *warm colors* bring objects closer, while *cool colors* make them appear more distant. If you paint a spot of medium blue next to a spot of yellow, you will see that the yellow "approaches," it is "located" in the foreground, while the blue "retreats," remains in a more distant plane. If you apply this formula of "near" and "far" colors to a painting, you will undoubtedly accentuate its depth.

Fig. 192—Including an object in the foreground whose size and dimensions we are familiar with, as in this case of a group of trees, creates the idea of distance between the foreground and the rest of the painting, giving the painting a third dimension, that is, depth.

Fig. 193—Depth can also be found in landscapes like this one in which the superimposition (or overlapping) of successive planes (see the adjoining sketch) facilitates the representation of depth.

Fig. 194—Any effect of perspective, in a street, a building, a road with trees, etc., gives the painting the impression of a third dimension, a representation of depth.

Fig. 195—Atmosphere and depth can be seen in paintings like this one, painted at eight o'clock in the morning, when the sun is rising and a golden mist surrounds the middle ground and background.

Fig. 196—Paint "near" colors in the foreground, such as yellow and orange. In the middle and background, paint "far" colors, such as greens and blues. In this way, you will highlight the depth almost automatically.

composition in practice

Finally, once in front of the model, keep in mind these three important rules to improve your watercolor's composition:

1. Approach the subject just enough to create a center of interest that "explains" the content or reason for the painting. Don't paint empty spaces, minimizing the elements that are the real reason for the painting. Approach without fear!

2. To decide how to frame the subject, take a cardboard frame (fig. 198) with you that will enable you to choose the best point of view, and thus, the best composition for the subject. Better yet, before beginning to paint, do a quick postcard-sized sketch suggesting the framing and composition of the subject.

3. Finally, don't be content with the subject as you first see it. Look at it from farther to the right, from farther to the left, stooping or climbing where you can, so that you have a chance to pick the best viewpoint.

197

198

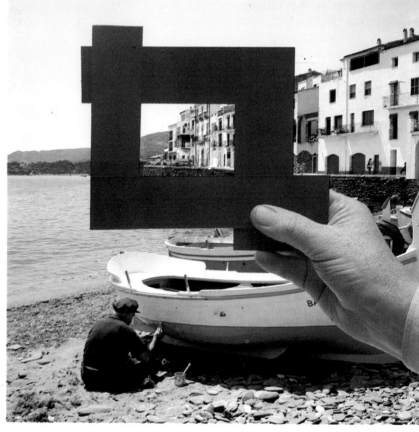

Figs. 197, 198—One of the most common mistakes made by the inexperienced amateur is to place himself too far away from the principal subject, losing the opportunity to emphasize the painting's center of interest. Note the difference in these figures between staying far away or drawing near the subject.

Fig. 199—Get a cardboard frame painted black or covered with black paper. With this frame, you will be able to study the framing of the subject before beginning to paint. Better yet, sketch a quick note with a lead pencil or watercolors to analyze the framing you have chosen and the composition in general.

Figs. 200, 201—Before beginning to paint, exhaust all possible points of view and framings. Try to get as much as you can out of these factors, which have such an impact on the painting's composition.

199

200

201

wash:
warm-up
for watercolor

characteristics and similarities

Learning to paint is always difficult. Painting watercolors is even more difficult. First of all, as in all the visual arts, you have to know how to draw very well. What's more, you must master color, and the compositions and mixtures of colors. As if this weren't enough, you must also know the *craft* of watercolor painting. Well then, "divide and conquer." It is a matter of dividing these three basic problems and reducing them, in principle, to just two: drawing and craft. These two problems can be studied separately, without going into the problem of color just yet, by practicing gouache painting, a true first step toward watercolor painting.

The examples here of gouache painting, done by Nicolas Poussin and John Constable, painted in two colors, one sienna and one black (or Payne's gray), allow us to compare the characteristics and similarities of gouache and watercolor. In these landscapes, note the transparency of the gouache and the absence of opaque white; the whites here are actually the white of the paper set off beforehand. The resolution runs from less to more, in other words, it was arrived at by superimposing dark layers over light, a typical characteristic of watercolor painting.

It is natural, therefore, for us to start these exercises by painting in gouache, and it makes sense to do it with colors as bright as red, blue, and yellow, as we will see in a minute.

Materials Needed

Watercolor paper (of good quality), heavyweight, as thick as necessary for mounting.

A drawing board.

Watercolor paints.

Two sable brushes, nos. 8, 12, or 14.

A wide "paletilla" or wash brush, no. 20 or 24.

A piece of natural sponge.

A roll of paper towels.

Two jars for water.

A cup or pan to dilute colors.

Pencil, eraser, etc.

Fig. 203—Nicolas Poussin, *Scene in the Forest,* Albertina, Vienna.

Fig. 204—John Constable, *The Old Bridge at Plat Ford,* Victoria and Albert Museum, London.

first practical exercises

Dry Wash in a Medium Tone

Fig. 205—Place the board at a slight angle. On your paper draw a square, approximately 25 X 15 cm (9" X 9") in pencil. Keep a scrap of paper ready for testing. In a small cup or one of the pans of the palette box, prepare a wash of a medium cobalt blue. Try to get a tone like the one in the example here. Load the brush with a lot of color and begin by painting a band 2 to 3 cm (1" to 1 1/4") wide at the top of the square.

Begin by painting from side to side horizontally. Work with a no. 12 brush. Careful with the amount of paint—it should be enough to spread evenly as you paint, but it should not be so much that it runs or drips.

205

Begin painting from side to side, horizontally; paint with a number 12 brush.

206

Fig. 206—Continue to maintain the moisture, working quickly. Keep displacing the wash, moving toward the bottom, painting horizontally, always leaving enough paint on the bottom edge. To control the accumulation of paint and to keep it from running; the board can be slanted as necessary.

Now paint vertically, from top to botton, keeping the brush loaded so that you are always painting in wet.

207

Fig. 207—When you reach the bottom of the square you will have some paint accumulated. Quickly blot the brush with a paper towel and absorb the paint accumulated at the bottom until you have a regular, uniform tone over the whole square.

The perfect harmony and uniformity in the color of a medium tone dry wash basically depends on, first, the quality of the paper, second, the slant of the board, and third, the brush and the amount of paint in it. Of course, there is no chance of retouching or redoing it.

first practical exercises

Dry Wash in Different Tones

Figs. 208 to 211—Here the object, as can be seen from the picture, is to paint four progressively lighter shades of carmine (crimson) colored wash.

First draw four rectangles 15 × 8 cm (9″ × 3″). Use the color rose madder or any crimson and keep a piece of paper handy for testing. Start with the darkest shade, loading the brush with intense but not opaque wash.

For both this shade and the following ones, keep in mind the instructions given on the previous page. The procedure is the same. The difficulty now rests in not only achieving washes of even tones but also obtaining a range of progressive tones. In order to do this, it is necessary to test the color or more accurately, the tone, each time before beginning to paint. Be careful with the amount of paint necessary for each tone, keeping in mind that it is better to err on the side of excess than on the side of insufficient color.

208

209

210

211

ry Graded Wash

g. 212—Sketch a square
me 15 × 15 cm (9″ × 9″)
d get ready to paint a graded
ash, with the color cadmium
d, or vermillion, in the area
ecified. Have a scrap of
per on hand for testing and
ep in mind that the success
a graded wash in gouache
watercolor depends to a
ge extent on the quantity of
ter in the brush when you
gin to paint. Let's see: begin
painting a band saturated
th color in the upper portion
the square.
art with a band of intense
lor running from side to side,
the top of the square.

Begin painting a band, of intense color, from side to side, on the upper part of the picture.

212

g. 213—Quickly now: Wash
e brush, drain it slightly on
e edge of the water jar and
ply it to the bottom half of
e red band, dissolving and
adating toward the bottom
ut painting from side to side
all times, horizontally. Put
essure on the brush to bring
ut more water, making sure
at the color does not accu-
ulate when you lift the brush.
lways paint horizontally. Move
ward the bottom rapidly,
utting pressure on the brush
release more water.

Always paint horizontally, descend rapidly pressing the brush to discharge more water.›

213

g. 214—Wash the brush
gain, drain it as before, and
ontinue gradating until you get
the bottom of the square.
ou will probably have to wet
d drain the brush during this
nal phase, controling the
mount of liquid, going over it,
etouching... but not too much,
nce if you paint and repaint,
eturning to the upper part of
e wash, the difficulties in-
rease and the gradation will
ot come out clean. You have
move quickly, measuring the
ater and working preferably
ith the bottom portion, which
this stage is the only area
at allows for repeating and
etouching.

214

first practical exercises

Wet Graded Wash

Fig. 215—The first step is to moisten the square or area to be painted using a natural sponge (a small piece of sponge such as the one in fig. 216), or a wide, flat, Japanese-style brush like the one mentioned previously in the chapter on supplies. This wetting of the paper should be done by rubbing the sponge over the paper lightly several times so that the paper's fiber does not deteriorate, but will absorb the moisture without water remaining on the surface. You should be painting on a damp, but not wet, surface. Work with the paper slanted at a 60 to 75 degree angle. Load the brush with yellow ochre, with less water than previously, and paint the top band of the picture. Half rinse the brush quickly, and continue gradating with quick strokes that do not alter the uniformity; move with spontaneity. Keep in mind that gradating the top part to the middle is the most difficult part. This is the hardest and most complicated exercise here, and you should not be surprised if it does not come out on the first try.

Painting with the Sponge

Fig. 216—Prepare a cup with the amount of wash (cobalt blue with a little ochre) needed to paint a cloudy sky some 18 × 25 cm (7″ × 10″). Wet the brush with clean water and moisten the paper with several strokes of the sponge and water.

Fig. 217—Squeeze out the sponge, load it with the color prepared in the cup and paint, pressing lightly, from side to side, controlling the evenness, squeezing the sponge more or less to extract more or less color.

Fig. 218—When you get to the bottom third, drain the sponge a bit, add a little clean water, and load it with gouache of a very light ochre color only. Paint using this slightly lighter color, mixing it and gradating it with the still-wet previous color, until you get to the horizon or the bottom edge of the rectangle.

Fig. 219—Still working wet, retouch the bottom part of the wash, controlling and retouching the evenness, absorbing gouache with the brush if necessary.

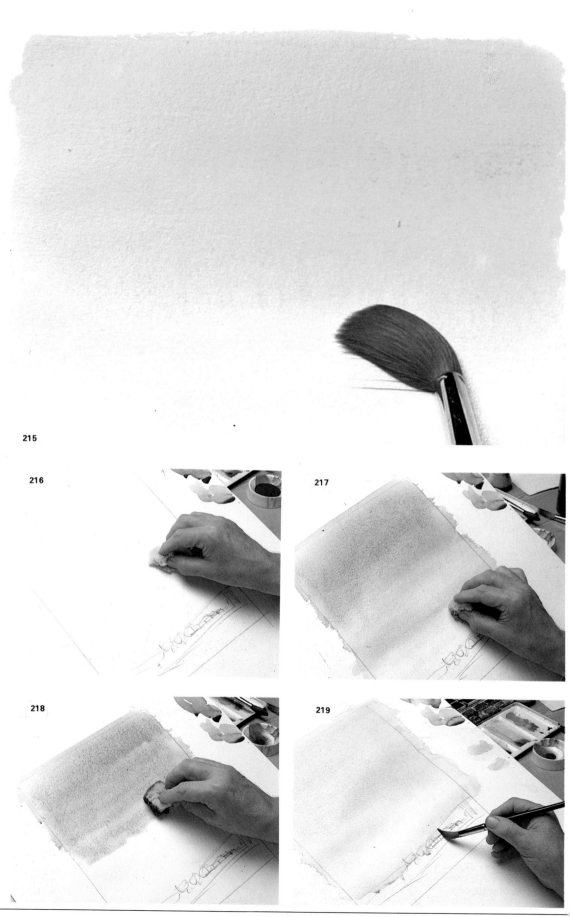

215

216

217

218

219

techniques of watercolor

In several pages I will ask you to paint in gouache using two colors. Since gouache is in many ways similar to watercolor, I would first like to go over some techniques for painting in

watercolor. I begin with the method used by professionals to "open up" whites, or to "erase" paint so the white of the paper is once more exposed.

220

Wet: This is how to "erase" still-wet wash and "open up" white space.
1. Begin by washing the brush and draining it with the help of a paper towel. 2. Apply the brush to the still wet

221

wash area, and you will observe that the brush absorbs the liquid and the color underneath. 3. If the white is not sufficiently light, wash the brush again, drain it once

222

more with the paper towel and apply it again. By repeating this operation several times you can obtain an almost perfect white.

223

Dry: Here it is a matter of "erasing" a wash that has already dried.
1. Begin by wetting the area with a brush and clean water. At the same time, rub gently with the end of the brush, diluting and lifting the color.

224

2. With a scrap of paper towel, folded in quarters or smaller, absorb the water applied previously. With this, you will begin to open up the white. Repeat the operation several times until you get a satisfactory white.

225

Extra help from bleach: To obtain a purer white you can use bleach diluted with water (half bleach, half water). But be careful: You should use a synthetic brush, the only kind that will withstand the corrosive effects of the bleach. Sable hair or others, such as ox hair or squirrel, will burn.

226

Comparing results: Wet: Undoubtedly the best of the techniques explained here, permitting even the painting of forms with gradated washes, forming for example the shapes of the clouds.

227

Dry: A laborious technique that, in the end, does not give good results. Absorption is more difficult with certain colors (carmine, emerald green, Prussian blue, and cadmiums in general resist being diluted).

228

With bleach: This technique is also laborious, but the results are clearly good, as can be seen in this illustration. It is difficult perhaps if attempting graded washes, since the bleach cuts the edges of the treated areas.

techniques of watercolor

How to reserve whites ahead of time

In watercolor white is provided by the white of the paper, there is no white paint. The ability of the good watercolorist is exhibited, among other things, by his knowing how to reserve the white areas ahead of time. However, sometimes reserved areas are small, thin, or situated on top of a uniform background. The professional will the use *masking fluid* or white wax, employing the techniques explained here.

229

Reserving with masking fluid: Once the drawing is done and the area or forms to be set off have been studied, one proceeds to paint them with masking fluid with a synthetic no. 4 brush. The masking fluid is of a light green or cream color, so that you can see where it has been applied.

230

2. Once the areas are reserved with masking fluid, you can paint over and around them without any limitations. The masking fluid rejects the water of the watercolor, and so continues to be visible.

231

3. When the artist is ready, the masking fluid is removed by rubbing it with a finger, uncovering the white paper. Naturally, this can be done when the watercolor has dried.

232

4. Then the reserved areas can be painted with the colors, lights, and shadows of the model, following the normal procedures for painting. Masking fluid is a good aid, but it is not advisable to abuse its use, since it never gives the same quality as the white reserved with the brush while painting.

233

Reserving with white wax: 1. White wax can also be used to reserve whites before beginning to paint. Once the drawing is completed and the whites that can be reserved before hand have been studied, you "paint" them in with a white wax crayon, with more or less fine

234

lines, depending on the shapes chosen.
2. Then you paint around these reserved shapes or areas, knowing that you can paint on top of the wax, since it will repel the water.

235

3. But be careful! If you go over the wax reserve again and again, it will finally absorb, either totally or partially, the liquid color, and the effect of the reserved white will disappear.

Other techniques to "open up" whites

The requirement that the white paper serve as white color, forces the artist to use a series of procedures for those cases in which the white was not reserved beforehand. These cases, usually unforseen, are solved by the professional with some of the techniques which are explained on this page.

Scrubbing out whites in dry paint: 1. When you want a white in a dark area in an already dry watercolor painting, it is advisable to do it with a synthetic flat brush, no. 4, which has stiffer bristles than sable hair. Begin by moistening the chosen area with lots of water.

2. Let the water sit for a minute or two, allowing it to soften the paper and the paint, and then rub softly with a clean, rinsed brush until the deposited water begins to get cloudy with the loosened paint. At that moment, dry the area with a paper towel.

3. For a purer white you can resort to bleach diluted with water and applied with a synthetic brush. Once the whitening is done you can paint again, retouching, creating shapes, etc.

Scratching out whites in wet paint with a bevelled brush handle: 1. There has always been a need in watercolor painting to create white lines against a dark background. This must be done in a freshly painted area, while the paint is still damp and the color is somewhat thick.

2. There are two ways to open up these white lines: one consists of tracing them forcefully and resolutely using the bevelled end of a special brush with a plastic handle and synthetic bristles, or...

with the fingernail. The other system, used by today's watercolorist and those of a hundred fifty years ago, is to scratch and expose the white paper with the nail of the pinky or ring finger in the form and position illustrated in this figure.

"Opening up" white spaces with a knife or blade (dry paint): The watercolor must be absolutely dry for this procedure. Here a white line can be etched from a dark background with the sharp edge of a mat knife, x-acto, or single-edge blade.

"Opening up" white spaces with sandpaper (dry paint): 1. With a small piece of very fine sandpaper (in this example 3/0 has been used) a perfect white can be "opened up" by vigorously rubbing the chosen area (the paint must be completely dry).

2. The success of a white obtained with sandpaper depends to a large extent on the quality of the watercolor paper. If it is thick and of good fiber it will survive and come out like new to be repainted on.

techniques of watercolor

Textures

The "frottis," the textural effects, the stains... The techniques of the watercolor are extremely varied and offer the possibility, within the purest forms of watercolor, of painting with systems (methods) and procedures that create diversity and style. We offer in this page some of these procedures, which I request you put into practice, in order to enrich (improve) your technique and your trade in watercolor.

245

"Frottis" or rubbing with the brush: 1. This technique, also called dry brush, consists of painting with an almost dry brush, which when rubbed, reproduces the rough texture of the paper, as seen in this illustration.

246

2. "Frottis" can be applied at edges and contours in a casual or premeditated way, as in this example.

247

3. The dry brush technique is also used to create contrast and to represent the rough texture of certain forms. In any case, it is advisable to try this technique out on a separate sheet of paper before using it.

248

Textural effects with water: 1. Painting with the wet watercolor technique, very rich textural effects can be achieved simply by loading the brush with clean water and applying it to a recently painted area that is still damp.

249

2. The spots and special effects which result from this wet-in-wet technique will suggest surprising textural effects to enrich the color and style of your painting.

250

Painting with a toothpick on a wet surface. With the aid of a stick or toothpick loaded with the watercolor from a brush, you paint and draw, defining lines, tree branches, etc. The moist paper dilutes the paint from the small stick, making it run and creating an original, modern idiom.

251

Transfer: 1.Transfer is a technique of pressing a recently painted and still wet paper against another paper that may be white or painted, wet or dry.The pressure will transfer the wet area, creating an abstract configuration or texture on the receiving paper. Transfer is used for background, walls, gorund, hills, etc.

252

2. Example of transfer: The paper to be painted on was painted a light blue. The transfer paper was painted an even, dark blue that, when applied, left this abstract image.

253

3. Another example of mackle: In this case the receptor paper (the painting), was painted a light yellow background, and the printing paper (the mackle) was painted with a crimson wash. When pressed, it printed this image.

Textures and special effects

On this page we find some special effects, such as those obtained with essence of turpentine and kitchen salt, which, when applied to the wet watercolor creates various textures and finishes that invite us to experiment, to invent, to create, and to discover a personal style, one's own visual language.

254

255

Textural effects with turpentine: 1. A synthetic brush is loaded with turpentine and brushed over a freshly painted, still damp area. When the turpentine comes into contact with the watercolor or gouache, light-colored, irregularly-shaped spots are formed, creating special effects and textures.

2. You can paint over areas treated with turpentine without difficulty, although it does not make sense to go over them with more watercolors to the point of eliminating or diminishing the effects achieved previously.

256

257

258

Textural effects with salt: 1. If you paint a medium-toned, even wash and sprinkle salt on it while it is still damp, you will see that as the paint dries the grains of salt absorb the pigment and form some curious spots, light in color, and diffused.

2. This effect can be used for the background, walls, ground, hills, etc., of a watercolor, creating special effects of surprising quality.

3. When this effect has been achieved in the areas treated with salt and the painting is dry, the grains of salt sticking to the painting can be removed simply by rubbing them gently with your fingers. In any case, you can paint over them without any problem.

259

260

261

Graded washes through dispersion or pointillism: 1. Here is an example whose sky has turned out too light, lessening the contrast between the ship's sail and the color of the sky. For this and other cases, it may be interesting to paint a gray area or wash with an air brush technique, but by hand.

2. The technique of pointillism consists of dragging a toothbrush loaded with color across the teeth of an ordinary comb. This dragging produces a spray of liquid watercolor. Naturally, before, it is necessary to cut a paper pattern to cover the shapes that are to be reserved.

3. Final results, and finishing off with marker, ball-point or India ink: Here are the results —the sky has gradually darkened, and the subject shows more contrast. Note further, the finishing black lines which have been added with a marker to emphasize some of the painting's contours and shapes.

painting with two colors

This is an exercise that I request you put into practice: paint with wash techniques using only two colors, from a model made of a cube, a cylinder and a glass of water on a table, against a white Bristol board as the background. Have I said two colors? Well, they aren't two, but four colors, namely:

> *Cobalt blue*
> *Burnt umber*
> *Black*
> *White*

In the enclosed fig. 262 and 263, you will see the blue, the brown, the black—created by mixing the blue and brown—and the white, which is simply the white of the paper. But there are still more colors, an infinite range of tones, which you can see here. Therefore, considering the range of colors that this particular palette can create, we might say that we are going to paint without limitations, with many colors, much like the original, renowned English watercolorists who used only to add a red ochre, in order to obtain beautifully colored paintings, and perfect color harmonies. Looking at fig. 267 on the next page you will notice the illumination of the model created by the small desk lamp and the white Bristol board background; fig. 266 shows you the setup.

Let me now ask you to construct the cube and cylinder out of light-weight Bristol board, following the design and measurements given in fig. 265. As for the glass, it doesn't matter if your glass is different from the model, but try to find a glass that, like the model, offers some decorative relief to make reflections, and variations.

Without any more introductions, this is how I painted the model.

Materials:

The two above mentioned colors.
Watercolor paper, 300 grams, fine grain.
Lead pencil (normal), no. 2.
Kneaded eraser and white plastic eraser.
Brushes of marten hair, nos. 8 and 12.
Masking fluid (liquid gum).
Absorbent paper.
Two containers with water.

262

263

264

Figs. 262, 263, 264—Only two colors are used in doing the practical exercises described on the following pages, cobalt blue and burnt umber. But in reality, you will also have the use of black, produced by mixing the two colors, and the white of the paper. Observe, in these illustrations, the wide range of colors and tones that you can obtain using just the two colors mentioned.

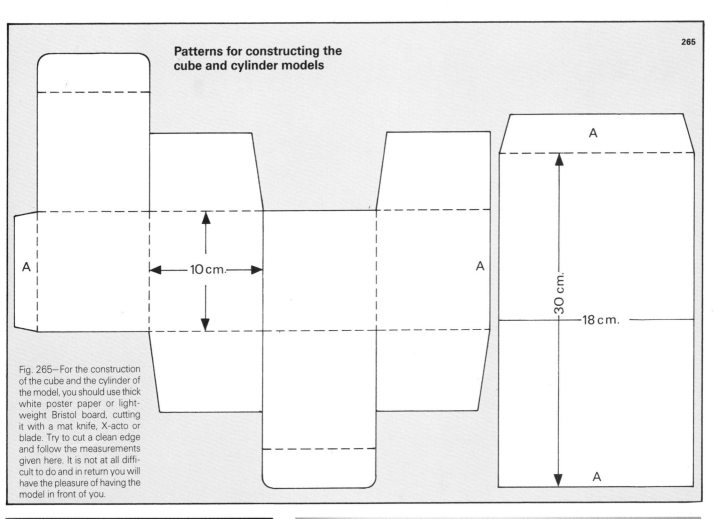

Patterns for constructing the cube and cylinder models

265

10 cm.

A

A

A

30 cm.

18 cm.

A

Fig. 265—For the construction of the cube and the cylinder of the model, you should use thick white poster paper or light-weight Bristol board, cutting it with a mat knife, X-acto or blade. Try to cut a clean edge and follow the measurements given here. It is not at all difficult to do and in return you will have the pleasure of having the model in front of you.

266

267

Figs. 266, 267—(Above) Note the position of the model and the type of lighting, coming from the side, from the table-top lamp. Note the white Bris-tol board behind the model as background, and to the right, the play of lights created by the model.

painting with two colors

First stage: drawing and reserving with masking fluid (Fig. 268)

For this relatively easy drawing, I begin with the cylinder, noting that its height is equal to twice its width, while the left profile of the glass is just in the center of the cube, and the diameter of the glass is slightly bigger than that of the cylinder, etc., etc. As usual, I draw without shadows, using only line. Once the drawing is complete, I reserve the bright areas of the glass, by painting them with the masking fluid and synthetic brush. Notice in fig. 268 the small color stains of the masking fluid which will allow me to find the reserved areas later on.

Second stage: painting the background (Fig. 269)

Using clean water and a sponge I wet the surface of the paper, to eliminate any possible residues of grease left by my hand while I was drawing. I wait for the moisture to dry before I wet the paper again, this time with the marten hair brush no. 12, and only in the background area behind the model, following carefully the contours of the cube and cylinder. Watch out! Don't go past the line or the color of the background will invade the shapes of the cube and the cylinder. Without allowing this new layer of water to dry, I paint the background warm gray, using a little more burnt umber than blue. I wait for a few minutes until this first paint wash dries. Then I paint the table, mixing blue and burnt umber with a predominance of the latter. But, pay attention: I don't paint with an absolutely regular and uniform wash. I mix the colors as I paint, at times mixing them on the paper itself, with the purpose of achieving a color with slight variations.

Third stage: painting the cylinder and cube (Fig. 270)

I go on to the cylinder. First wetting the visible part with water, reserving the part half hidden by the glass, and then painting over the still-moist area with a wash with a slightly bluish tendency. I charge the brush and, with a slightly zig-zagging stroke, I paint a dark stripe from the top to the bottom of the cylinder, still reserving the part hidden by the glass. Fast now! With the brush cleaned and a little wrung out, we have to dilute the previous color in the shadowy area, by degrading it as it moves toward the illuminated zone. I paint the side of the cube which is most in shadow, using a premixed wash. When the facing square has dried, I paint it a cold clearer gray color.

268

269

Fig. 268—The first stage of this two-color painting exercise shows the drawing done in pencil and the small colored spots of masking fluid, indicating the points where whites have been reserved.

Fig. 269—In this second stage, it is important to achieve the irregular color of the table, with small variations that better reflect reality. The graded wash of the background, behind the geometric shapes, has been painted wet-in-wet.

Next, I paint the triangular shadow projected by the cube on the cylinder. And before it dries, soften the edges of the shadow so that it does not look so hard. I finally paint the shadow on the inside of the cylinder.

Fourth stage: the glass, shadows projected on the table, and some finishing touches (Fig. 271)
I first paint with diluted gouache, indicating the construction form and slight variations of tone in the glass. While this dries I go to the background, darkening the area behind the angle formed by the edges of the cylinder and the cube, and paint wet-in-wet. Next I remove the masking fluid and retouch some of the uncovered white areas. I paint the shadows projected by the model on the table; when I reach the shadow of the glass, I have opened up a small spot of white to represent the light reflected by the glass's crystal surface. Finally, I work on the lights and shadows of the glass, thus finishing this study.

270

271

Fig. 270—Third stage; the graded wash of the cylinder has been painted wet-in-wet, that is, wetting the paper beforehand with clean water. Observe the tenuous but visible light reflected in the face of the cube more than in its shadow and note that at this stage, the cylinder's shadow can also be seen through the glass.

Fig. 271—Removing the masking fluid by rubbing with the finger and uncovering the pure whites reserved previously is always a surprise... at times an unpleasant one because of the excessive contrast and the need to paint and retouch, to soften the harsh contrasts of the color and the whites. Try, as I have done, to enrich the color, diversifying tones and shades and painting blues, remembering that blue is visible in the glass, in the shadows, etc. Finally, note the black lines, drawn with ballpoint, that mark the bases of the cube and the inside edges, in the shadow, of the cube and the cylinder.

examples in wash

Fig. 272—Wash painting, even painting with only black watercolor or diluted India ink, offers ample possibilities for artistic expression. In addition, it is a perfect medium for getting started in the practice of watercolor painting. These pictures show an excellent wash painting of a landscape by Federico Lloveras, and a sketch I made of a child's head.

theory and practice in colors

primary, secondary and tertiary colors

To summarize:

Nature "paints" with the *colors of light.* Newton, the physicist, reproduced the phenomenon of the rainbow: in a dark room he intercepted a light beam with a crystal prism, and was thus able to *decompose* the white light into the six colors of the spectrum. Young, another famous physicist, did the opposite: while doing research with colored lamps, he was able to *recompose* light, obtaining white light. Besides this, he arrived at the important conclusion that the six colors of the spectrum could be reduced to three basic colors, from which he established the *three basic light colors:* green, red, and dark blue. By mixing these three *light colors* in pairs, Young determined the *three secondary light colors:* cyan blue; purple; and yellow. To summarize: everything that you and I are seeing right now, is receiving the three basic light colors and, through extension, the three secondary light colors. Nature "paints" with light colors.

In the studio we paint with pigment colors. Fortunately we paint with the same colors, with the difference that we change the value or primacy of some colors with reference to others, and we can thus say that:

**Our primary colors
are the secondary light colors.
Our secondary colors
are the primary light colors.**

Primary pigment colors (secondary light colors)

Yellow, Cyan Blue[1], Purple

Secondary pigment colors (primary or basic light colors), by paired mixture of the previous colors:

Red, Green, Dark Blue

Pigment color mixing is always supposed to *subtract light,* that is to say, to pass on from light to dark colors: if we mix red and green we get a darker color—brown. We get black if we mix our three primary colors together. Physicists call this phenomenon: *subtractive synthesis.* Light, in turn, "paints" by *adding colors:* by adding a red beam to a green beam the amount of light is duplicated, and logically we obtain a clearer light, in this case yellow. This phenomenon is called *additive synthesis.*

Now look at the chromatic circle or table of pigment colors—our colors— derived from the

three *primary* colors (P), which, mixed in pairs, produce the three *secondary* colors (S), which, if mixed with the primary colors, make six more colors known as *tertiary* colors (T).

What we have seen and read up until now, leads us to the following practical conclusions, which justify our knowledge of the theories on color:

—Light and the artist "paint" with the same colors: the colors of the spectrum.

—The perfect coincidence between light colors and pigment colors permits the artist to imitate the effects of light as it illuminates forms and to reproduce with great fidelity, all the colors of nature.

—In accordance with the theories of light and color, the artist can paint all of the colors of Nature, with only three primary colors: cyan blue, purple, and yellow.

---

(1) The term cyan blue does not appear in the color charts for watercolor or oil paints. It belongs to the graphic arts and color photography, and has been adopted by the present for the purpose of discussing color theory. It corresponds to a neutral blue, very similar to Prussian blue when mixed with a tinge of white.

Fig. 274—The decomposition of light, discovered by Newton, gives place to the formation of the spectrum composed of six basic colors.

Fig. 275—Colors of light: additive synthesis.

Fig. 276—Pigment colors: subtractive synthesis.

complementary colors

The enclosed chromatic color wheel shows the colors are complements of each color by pairing the colors one in front of the other. We thus see that:

Yellow is the complement of **Blue**
Cyan Blue is the complement of **Red**
Purple is the complement of **Green**
(and vice versa)

But, what is the use of knowing color complements?
In order to create color contrasts; to know, for example, that green next to red will make a really extraordinary contrast.
In order to paint with a different range of colors: a range of warm colors, cool colors, or broken colors, about which we will speak in the following pages.
In order to paint the color of shadows which we will discuss on the next page.

277

Fig. 277—The juxtaposition of complementary colors creates the maximum contrast of color. The mixture of two complementary colors becomes a dusty black. When the mixture is not in the proper proportions, you get a range of broken colors, or a range of grayish colors when working with watercolors.

Fig. 278—Chromatic circle or table of pigment colors, in which the primary colors (indicated with a P) appear. Mixed together in pairs they yield the three secondary colors (S), which when mixed in pairs one primary and one secondary yield six tertiary colors (T). The smaller circle shows the paired complementary colors indicated with arrows. Below is the list and classification of these colors.

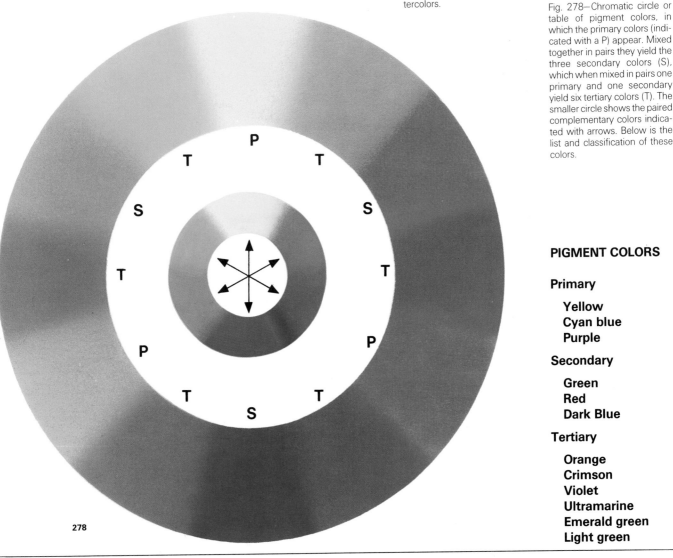

278

PIGMENT COLORS

Primary

    Yellow
    Cyan blue
    Purple

Secondary

    Green
    Red
    Dark Blue

Tertiary

    Orange
    Crimson
    Violet
    Ultramarine
    Emerald green
    Light green

the color of forms; the color of shadows

What's the color of things?

Well, people say that bananas are yellow, that tomatoes are red, and that some flowers are blue, but in fact, to us painters, these and all forms basically offer three factors which determine their color:

The local color or color of the object itself: the yellow of the bananas, the red of the tomatoes, that is to say, the intrinsic color, not modified by light, shadow or the reflection of other colors.

The tonal color: lighter or darker than the inherent color, it is due to the effects of light and shadow that lighten or darken the yellow of the bananas, the red of the tomatoes.

The ambiance or surrounding color resulting from various factors: the colors reflected from the colors of surrounding objects; the color of the light illuminating the forms which may be more or less orange, or blue; the intensity of the light; and the effects of the interposed atmosphere, which, as you know, diffuses light and modifies colors, giving forms a grayish hue.

But in the end the color of the form is there, in the model, and we have nothing to do other than observe carefully and follow its dictates. The biggest problem, the one that many amateurs (and some professionals) have not been able to grasp, is the color of shadows. What's the color of shadows? Is there a formula that would allow us to successfully solve the problem of painting the color of shadows? I think so.

The color of the shadow is constituted by:

1. **The color blue, which is present in all darkness.**
2. **The local color in a darker tonality.**
3. **The complementary of the local color.**

Let's use some examples:

The color blue, present in all darkness (fig. 279): this is certainly the most important of the three mentioned factors. Right from the beginning of the painting it is important to incorporate blue into the color of the shadow.

The local color in a darker tonality (fig. 280): the *tonal color,* Sienna appears in the shadow of yellow; carmine in that of red.

The complementary of the local color (fig. 281): Blue complements yellow; green complements red or carmine, and so on.

How you mix these colors, what proportion of each you choose, depends on whether you want to paint in a classic or modern style

Fig. 279—If we could make a dissection of the colors that are in any shadow, we would see that, as in this peach, blue is present in all the colors, but in greater quantities in shadowed areas.

Fig. 280—In the same manner, the local or intrinsic color is present in the shadow, but in a darker tone. Before Impressionism, which gave voice to this rule, artists resolved the color of the shadows by adding brown or gray.

Fig. 281—Ever since the Impressonist movement, and following the laws of Chevreul, the complement of the color of the object being painted is present in its shadow. If the intrinsic local color is red, there is green in the shadow.

Fig. 282—Mixing the colors mentioned in the figures above gives us the color of the shadows, with a marked approximation to reality. The artist will of course vary the proportions and quantities of color to respond to his or her own style.

colorists and value painters

—more classic if you accentuate the darker tonality of the local color, and more modern if the tendency is bluer, mixing blue with the complement of the local color. In either case, you will have solved the problem of the color of shadows. That's what I hope.

Some artists paint almost completely with flat color without shadow,especially in contemporary painting. Have you noticed this? These are the artists that Andre Lhote classified as *colorists:* "those who rely mainly on color"; those who, while painting outdoors, choose frontal illumination or diffused lighting without shadows, seeing and differentiating forms with color reminiscent of the style of some of the old masters such as Fra Angelico, Hieronymus Bosch, the Brueghel brothers. And color as form was a basic principle to the Impressionists and fauvists from Van Gogh to Matisse to Derain, with their premeditated exploitation of color, because, as Bonnard wrote, "color alone, without any help, is capable of representing mass and volume, and of expressing a pictorial climate."

On the other side are the value painters, those artists who paint the model with lights and shadows, who use the natural shadow (shadow of the form itself) and the projected shadow to explain volume. In this group can be included all the classical painters and some as modern as Corot, Courbet, Nonell, and Dali. It seems obvious that the colorist is closer to the formulas and styles of the present—if it is true that "there are neither good nor bad styles," as Andre Lhote said, "only good or bad ways of using them." On the other hand there is no reason why one should follow a single formula: Picasso would sometimes paint with flat color devoid of shadows, while at other times he would yield the role of protagonist to shading, modeling, mass and volume. "To paint? To draw?" Cézanne said. "When the color appears in all its richness, the form appears in all its plenitude." But the question remains: you now know the two alternatives, will you then paint as a colorist or a value painter?

283

284

Fig. 283—Federico Lloveras. *El Pilar, Zaragoza,* private collection. An example of value painting. The artist attempts to resolve and explain the forms of objects through the use of light and shadow—a classical style of painting, used by most artists throughout the last century.

Fig. 284—Federico Lloveras, *Fishing Port in the North of Spain,* private collection. Here, the same artist paints in the style of the colorist. Forms are not rendered by pattern or by the play of lights and shadow, but rather through the use of color: the different colors of each house, each boat, each object. Modern painting contains many examples of the *colorist* interpretation, particularly among the art of the Fauvists and Expressionists.

harmony

In 1840, at the age of sixty-five, Turner traveled for the second time to Venice, where he painted the best watercolors of his life time. They were, and still are, a marvel of technique, a fabulous mastery of water and color, but above all, a masterly lesson on mixing and harmonizing color. Looking at the extraordinary beauty of Venice painted with grays and blues, the great Constable said of Turner's work: "He has been able to dye the atmosphere." Turner did not arrive at these results by chance. It's certain that the resolution of these famous watercolors, responds to a preconceived idea of color tendency or color dominance, that Turner would then develop into a range of colors: "A succession of perfectly organized colors or tonalities."

In fact, a painting can be completely toned with colors of a blue tendency by using a *range of cold colors;* or it may be painted with a red tendency by using a *range of warm or hot colors;* in the same manner, it may offer a series of grayish tones and colors, through the use of a *range of broken colors.*

Fortunately for us, the artists, these color ranges appear in the model itself, thanks to the fact that in Nature there exists always, no matter what the theme may be, a *luminous tendency,* which causes a relationship between colors. At times, this tendency is very accentuated. For example, at daybreak on a foggy day when blue and gray dominate, or at sunset when everything is golden, yellow, and red. When the harmonizing of colors is not so evident, the artist must plan and organize; accentuate, exaggerate... imagine a color tendency and hold onto it with a true obsession, from the moment he starts painting to the finishing touches.

Do it this way, and perhaps you too will be able to "dye the atmosphere."

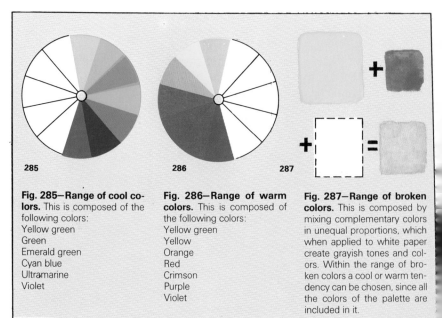

285   286   287

Fig. 285—Range of cool colors. This is composed of the following colors:
Yellow green
Green
Emerald green
Cyan blue
Ultramarine
Violet

Fig. 286—Range of warm colors. This is composed of the following colors:
Yellow green
Yellow
Orange
Red
Crimson
Purple
Violet

Fig. 287—Range of broken colors. This is composed by mixing complementary colors in unequal proportions, which when applied to white paper create grayish tones and colors. Within the range of broken colors a cool or warm tendency can be chosen, since all the colors of the palette are included in it.

288

289

Fig. 288—Turner. *Venice: The Great Channel.* British Museum. London. One of Turner's watercolors, painted during his second trip to Venice, this offers an example of a range of cool colors.

Fig. 289—Whistler. *Gray and Green. A shop in England.* Glasgow University. Donated by Birnie Philip. A good example of a subject painted with a palette of broken colors of grayish tendency.

color mixing
in watercolor

three basic colors

Light, Color, Pigments, Primaries, Secondaries...
No, no. We're not going to continue talking about color theories, but rather, the practical application of these theories, which, as we said before, allow us to make the fabulous discovery of Newton and Young so that we may:

Paint all the colors of Nature with only three colors.

The three primary pigment colors—yellow, cyan blue, and purple—mixed in pairs, give us the secondaries, green, red, and dark blue and all six, mixed in pairs give us the tertiaries, and so on and on.
The equivalent in watercolor or gouache of these three magic colors is:

Cadmium yellow medium
Prussian blue
Alizarin crimson carmine
(Plus the white of the paper)

Fig. 291—Here is a watercolor note that I myself did painting with only three colors, cadmium yellow medium, Prussian blue, and rose madder.

291

Fig. 292—A. Graded wash of cadmium yellow medium.

B. Graded wash of cyan blue.

C. Graded wash of alizarin crimson carmine.

Fig. 293—A. The mixture of the primary colors yellow and blue gives green.

B. The range of greens that can be obtained by mixing yellow and blue is practically infinite.

Fig. 294—A. Mixing carmine and yellow, we obtain red.

B. Note the wide range of reds, oranges, and yellows that can be obtained by mixing crimson and yellow.

Fig. 295—A. Blue mixed with purple gives us an intense blue of violet tones.

B. With cyan blue and purple a wide range of carmines, purples, and violets can be achieved.

Fig. 296—A. When the three primary colors are mixed together, they produce black.

B. This is the range of grays that is obtained with the black produced by mixing the three primary colors.

warm colors

1 2 3 4 5 6

7 8 9 10 11 12

13 14 15 16 17 18

297

This exercise will serve as the preamble to a whole watercolor painted with these three colors.
You will need the following materials:
Medium grain paper, 250 grams or more, of good quality.
The three colors mentioned above.
Palette or palette-box.
Brush of marten hair no. 8.
Roll of absorbent containers paper.
Two containers with clean water.
Please read the following instructions referring to the numbered samples above, together they will provide you with instructions for composing a vast range of colors.

1. *Lemon Yellow:* Composed with only cadmium yellow and water.
2. *Light rose yellow for skin tone:* Composed with the above and a very small wash of carmine.
3. *Pink yellow:* The previous color with a bit more carmine.
4. *Light orange:* Intense cadmium yellow with a little bit of carmine..

5. *English red:* Intense charge of yellow and carmine.
6. *Vermilion:* Intense charge of carmine with a bit of yellow.
7. *Pink:* Carmine with abundant water.
8. *Light carmine:* Wash of intense carmine.
9. *Purple:* Wash of carmine with a bit of Prussian blue.
10. *Light yellow ochre:* First a wash with more yellow than carmine; then add little by little a small quantity of blue.
11. *Dark yellow ochre:* Same as the previous, but increasing the yellow and the blue.
12. *Natural Sienna:* First an orange (4. or 6. above) and little by little add blue.
13. *Burnt Sienna:* Compose an intense purple; then add yellow.
14. *Van Dyck brown:* A thick mixture of intense blue and yellow; then add carmine until you achieve this warm dark maroon.
15. *Warm bottle green:* Charge of in-

tense blue, a little carmine and yellow.
16. *Light gray of warm tendency:* Lots of water, a very light purple, and a clear wash of yellow.
17. *Dark gray of warm tendency:* Compose a dark purple of blue tendency; little by little add yellow.
18. *Black:* Thick amounts of blue and carmine will render an almost black color; add a little yellow for a warm black.

warm colors

We continue painting with warm colors, but we now incorporate greens and even blues into our mixes, since in a range of warm colors nuances of cold colors may intervene, that is "cold" colors with a warm tendency. Thus, this green will reflect a bit of red or Sienna, and here the blue will show a nuance of brown or carmine.

19. *Yellow green:* Wash of yellow with a bit of blue.
20. *Permanent green:* A neutral color neither cold nor warm, which you may compose simply with yellow and blue.
21. *Olive green:* The previous color with a bit of carmine.
22. *Dark green or emerald green:* Undiluted blue and yellow, the latter in smaller quantities, plus a touch of carmine.
23. *Grayish blue:* A wash of blue mixed with a very light wash of carmine.
24. *Darker gray blue:* The same as the previous, increasing the amounts.
25. *Warm bluish gray:* First compose a

wash of bluish green with lots of water, then add a wash of carmine.
26. *Dark warm gray:* The same as the above but increasing the amounts.
27. *Khaki:* Bluish green and a bit of carmine.
28. *Warm clear gray:* A very clear watery wash or blue and green and a still lighter (more watery) wash of carmine. (It is preferable with colors as liquid as this one, to mix on a clean palette or test paper).
29. *Light purple:* Wash of carmine and blue with an addition of some very light yellow wash.
30. *Neutral gray:* Wash of all three colors in equal amounts, but with a little more blue.
31. *Dark yellow green:* Somewhat intense yellow, a little bit of blue, and a very light wash of carmine.
32. *Natural Sienna:* The same composition as that in the previous color adding a bit of carmine.
33. *Venice red:* Identical composition as color number 32 with a bit more carmine.

34. *Burnt umber:* Now add a bit of blue wash to the composition of the previous color.
35. *Light burnt umber:* The previous color with more water and a bit more blue, that is, clearing and dirtying at the same time.
36. *Dark neutral gray:* Compose a neutral gray like that in fig. 30; slightly increase the amount of each color.

299

Fig. 299—Ceferino Olivé, *Plaza del teatro (Barcelona),* private collection. A notable example of color harmony in a warm range.

cold colors

37. 38. 39. 40. 41. 42.

43. 44. 45. 46. 47. 48.

49. 50. 51. 52. 53. 54.

300

We are now going to mix a range of cold colors with grays, blues, greens, and violets predominating, but without eliminating the yellow, reds, and Sienna, which may exist in an ensemble of cold colors, provided they retain a green-blue-gray tendency.

37. *Light blue:* Simply a blue wash with abundant water.
38. *Sky blue with warm tendency:* Blue wash mixed with a very light yellow wash.
39. *Sky blue of red or carmine tendency:* A blue wash with abundant water, mixed with carmine wash.
40. *Medium neutral gray:* The three colors equally distributed, with a slightly larger amount of blue.
41. *Light cold gray:* The previous color increasing the blue a little.
42. *Dark cold gray:* First compose a purple of medium intensity with a heavy load of color; add a bit of yellow and neutralize again with carmine and blue.
43. *Medium blue:* Simply a wash of very intense blue.
44. *Meadow green:* Blue and a bit of yellow with a heavy load of both colors.
45. *Blue green:* Composed with blue and yellow, loaded more with blue.
46. *Navy blue:* Prussian blue with much paint and little water.
47. *Violet:* Prussian blue and intense carmine.
48. *Bluish carmine (or dark carmine):* An intense wash of carmine with a little blue.
49. *Light earth green:* Compose an orange with yellow and carmine; little by little add blue.
50. *Dark earth green:* The same as the previous color with increased amounts of each color to make it darker.
51. *Dirty orange:* Mix yellow and carmine to make an orange, then add a bit of blue which will "cool" it off.
52. *Sienna:* Compose a wash with carmine and yellow to make a light red; then add a bit of blue.
53. *Dark lemon yellow:* Can the yellow color belong to a cold gamut? Yes. It is a yellow with bluish tendency, with a little bit of blue, which gives us a yellow closer to the cold range.
54. *Cold black:* A thick load of Prussian blue, a smaller quantity of carmine, and a little yellow. Increase the blue if necessary, in order for the blue tendency to become evident.

301

broken colors

Here we have a range of broken colors, worn out colors, close to gray or "dirty" colors. Some colors, you will remember, are the product of the mixture of two complementaries in unequal amounts and white. In watercolor the white is the paper, so the first part of the formula is enough.

55. *Light yellowish gray:* Using plenty of water, mix blue and carmine to make a violet blue, then add a bit of yellow (violet blue or purple is the complementary of yellow).
56. *Medium yellowish gray:* The same composition with higher amounts of color.
57. *Dark yellowish gray:* This is a good color to practice the combination of complementaries mixed in unequal proportions. On the one hand the blue and the carmine when mixed give us the violet blue, and on the other, the complementary yellow is added in smaller quantities. When we add the white of the paper, the broken color appears.

58. *Light gray carmine:* Compose a light green and add a wash of carmine.
59. *Medium gray carmine:* Same as the previous procedure, increasing the amounts slightly.
60. *Dark gray with a carmine tendency:* Compose a very clean green with a heavy load of color and slowly add carmine until you get to this color.
61. *Ochre:* Begin with a clean orange wash; then mix in blue in increasing amounts until you arrive at this color.
62. *Olive green:* Compose a clean green in a medium intense wash; little by little add carmine until you arrive at this color.
63. *Light sepia:* Compose a brilliant green with enough paint aud slowly add carmine.
64. *Intense sepia:* As the previous but using more color and finally adding either a little more blue or carmine.
65. *Grayish blue:* A blue wash with little carmine and even less yellow.
66. *Broken green yellow:* Begin with a

very clear yellow wash; add a wash of carmine and blue.
67. *Broken sky blue:* Prepare a very clean blue wash and add a very clear wash of carmine and yellow.
68. *Greyish blue:* The same colors as in the previous but in a more intense wash.
69. *Light neutral gray:* Mix washes of the three colors, composing in layers on the test paper, so that the three colors interact in equal proportions.
70. *Medium neutral grey:* Like the previous procedure, using larger quantities.
71. *Payne's gray:* A neutral grey with bluish tendency, this is made with intense blue, a bit of carmine, and less yellow.
72. *Neutral gray:* Intense thick blue, to which is added a bit of carmine and a bit less yellow. Test it before painting, because the actual nuance is not appreciated without seeing it on white paper.

"special" colors

Sometimes amateurs with little experience will ask: Is there a special color to paint silver or gold? What colors should one mix in order to paint crystal?

Let me answer these questions by saying that there aren't special colors to paint silver, there isn't a gold color, nor is there a color to paint crystal objects.

Crystal does not have color: To paint a crystal object is more complicated than painting a cube, but not more difficult. If anything, it is more laborious (painful), more time consuming: You have to observe the model attentively and consciously; you have to study the forms, transparencies, tonalities, and colors. "One has to stupidly copy everything," as the great Michelangelo used to say. There is no secret, or any special ability: the colors we see through a crystal object or reflected on their surfaces, are as concrete as those of a table or an apple. What happens is that these surfaces appear to vary in brightness and are broken by reflections; this slightly modifies the tonality of certain colors, and sometimes promotes small deformations, but that's all.

And the color gold does not exist: If we had to determine the local color of gold, we would certainly choose yellow ochre to begin with. But gold without brilliance or reflections would stop being gold. The color gold is the result of an ensemble of nuances, stains and small degradations, that can go from white to black (depending on the colors that the gold may reflect), passing through carmines, greens, Siennas, ochres, reds, yellows, blues, etc.

A

B

C

303

Fig. 303—Glass has no color. This glass receptacle (A) is white because it is placed in front of a white background which we see through the transparent glass. The same receptacle, placed in front of a red and orange background (B), appears to have these colors, with the edge of the colors slightly deformed by the shape of the receptacle. Against a black background a glass object (C) is physically recognized by the reflections of the lights and colors around it.

304

305

Fig. 304—Here is a basic range of colors for painting a gold object.

Fig. 305—With this range of colors I have painted the subject on the right. As you can see there is no gold color, but there is a series of colors and shades which, viewed and copied precisely, allow us to represent a gold object.

painting a watercolor with three colors

If you have painted the color ranges as I proposed to you in the last few pages, you're now ready to use the same three colors to paint a still life that you can prepare yourself. This is a very profitable exercise for anyone that paints watercolors: it reminds us of the importance of the three primary colors, and affirms the idea that in order to paint it is not necessary to use a wide range of colors.
But let's do it, let's paint.
Choose the objects that will compose your still-life painting. Try to compose a *motif,* not a theme; thinking about an original image, place the objects on top of a table, in an apparently casual arrangement. But let this arrangement respond, insofar as possible, to a concrete scheme of composition. I have tried to follow this road: I have positioned the objects of the model in a triangular scheme. I have made up my mind, besides, to paint as a *colorist,* using a range of cold colors, factors that may be guessed from the enclosed picture of the model. (fig. 306).

First stage: drawing and serving with masking fluid (Fig. 307)

First I do a test sketch, which I afterwards redraw with more precision; I draw without shading, using only lines made with a no. 2 pencil. Next, using synthetic hair brush no. 4, I cover and reserve some white areas with masking fluid. Pay attention to this point, there are two aspects that I want to underline: First, masking fluid is a means, not an end. Use it as a resource, but do not abuse it. As we will see shortly, it is much better to reserve whites by leaving out paint, than using the masking fluid. Second, apply the masking fluid with a great deal of care, anticipating the *situation and exact dimension* of the white space. As you know, masking fluid has a color, it is visible, and is therefore easy to apply.

Second stage: general tinting in the background and large areas (Fig. 308)

I begin by wiping the entire surface with a damp sponge with clean water, in order to eliminate any possible residues of grease left by my hand when I was drawing. Once it's dry, I again wet the background area behind the fruit bowl and water jar, using a brush made of marten hair, no. 12 (I paint with the drawing board slanted about 60 degrees on a desk easel). I mix a cold gray for the background. As I apply it, I mix in strokes of blue, carmine and yellow, mixing and varying the original gray

306

307

right on the paper. I continue with the light gray-blue-green of the table cloth, making it darker in the foreground, and attempting, as well, to enrich and diversify the color (notice how I have bypassed the top edge of the wine glass and jar); and I end up tinting with washes some of the larger areas such as the apple and the fruit dish.

Fig. 309—(Right): Using masking fluid, I reserve only the objects made of glass and ceramic. Nevertheless, when the rubber fluid is lifted off, the awful blanks constitute an unpleasant surprise, and throw doubt on the use of the liquid rubber.

Third stage: color intensifying color, modeling, removing the masking fluid (Fig. 309)

I now paint the bright colors of the fruit in flat tones without shadows, as well as the fruit dish, also as a colorist. I paint the lone apple. With cold grays I model the wine glass and the water jar. Next, I tear off the masking fluid by rubbing with my finger at the same time erasing the residue of lead pencil. Observe the state of the watercolor in fig. 309, and note the sharp contrast of the forms reserved with masking fluid. These will require retouching to smooth some edges and soften transitions with glazes.

Fourth and last stage: general adjustment of color and finishing touches (Fig. 310)

I have begun by painting some glazes (very clear washes) harmonizing some of the scandalous whites reserved by the masking fluid in the reflections in the jar and wine glass. In the

308

309

310

luminous halos of the fruit, the fruit dish, and the apple. Next, I reinforced the color of the fruit dish, adjusting some of the colors. I finish modeling the wine glass and jar. Be careful there! It would be fun to compose a general gray color and to paint everything with the same color. But on the contrary, we have to change and diversify the colors, accentuating the warm and cool tendencies offered by the model. Last, I finish the wrinkles of the table cloth in the foreground. Before signing it I

spend a day without looking at the painting. It is always true that the next day there is something one hadn't seen, something that could be improved. I have only painted with the three primary colors: cadmium yellow, medium, Prussian blue, and alizarin crimson carmine. I have worked on 300 gram paper, mounted on a block, and I have painted with moist watercolors in tubes and brushes of marten hair nos. 8, 12, and 14.

Fig. 310—If you have painted a watercolor like this, using your own model and composition, it will probably be difficult for your family and friends to believe that you painted with only three colors. You will have to prove to them that it is true and convince them that in fact, with only three colors, it is possible to paint all the colors that are found in nature.

technique
and skills

dry watercolors, wet watercolors

Dry painting is basically painting with transparent paints, using the white of the paper, and defining the contours and limits of the objects where called for by the model. This does not mean eliminating the breakdown or diffusion of cylindrical or spherical objects, nor does it call for painting the background in absolutely clear-cut and defined terms, as the latter would mean doing away with atmospheric effects.

Of course, dry painting involves the risk of the watercolors separating (see fig. 312), because the wash may dry while painting.

Dry painting with watercolors must progress from less to more, painting the light sections first, which may be used to finish large areas, and then applying darker coats.

Well then, if you look closely you will agree that *dry watercolor painting is like classical watercolor painting,* with no particular special technique: in fact, when someone uses the term "dry watercolor" they are differentiating it from "wet watercolor" because the latter does indeed require special techniques.

The technique for wet watercolor painting consists basically of painting on damp paper, so that the limits and contours of the objects appear diffused and not clearly defined. This lack of definition also appears in interior forms or profiles. The two paintings shown on the following page explain the technique of damp watercolor painting better than words.

The degree of dampness is a basic factor: the greater the dampness, the more the colors will run and the greater the effect of "bleeding" or lack of definition, and vice-versa. Therefore, one must control the degree of dampness, by moistening with the brush or by absorbing and decreasing the dampness with an absorbent paper towel. Remember, one must paint on damp, but not wet, paper. An artist friend of mine who is an expert in this technique told me: "One must always be watching the paper from an angle that shows the reflections: if the surface shines then there is too much water and one cannot paint. The surface is perfect when it has totally absorbed the water but is not yet dry."

Damp watercolor painting is recommended for painting landscapes or seascapes on gray days, for urban scenes on rainy days, for fog, and so on.

312

Fig. 312—Here is a watercolor with a *break* in it; a consequence of having been painted without the necessary continuity.

Fig. 313—Guillem Fresquet, *Naturaleza muerta,* private collection. This is a classic watercolor or *dry* watercolor. As such, the boundaries and outlines of the objects are clearly delineated, but to create atmosphere the artist has toned down the shapes in the background.

313

wet watercolors

Fig. 314—Aida Corina, *Marsh* (First medal at the XLVII Autumn Exhibition, Madrid). Swamps and marshes on plains like this are an excellent subject for painting wet in watercolors, beautifully achieved in this picture, which combines diffused shapes without boundaries with a number of concrete profiles, and some foreground shapes which are perfectly defined.

314

Fig. 315—J. Martin Anton, *Still Life*, private collection. The undeniable artistic quality of this watercolor stems in large part from the use of the wet-in-wet technique. The author, a teacher, painted this watercolor as a demonstration for a course organized by the Catalan Association of Water Color Painters.

315

synthesis

Giorgio Vasari, the fabulous chronicler of the Renaissance, compared the styles of Donatello and Luca della Robbia this way when writing in 1550: "The same feeling of beauty and vigor may frequently be observed in those rapid drawings which arise out of creative frenzy and are achieved with a minimum of lines, while an excess of industry and patience on the part of the artist who will not leave well enough alone robs the work of force and freshness."

In all periods, but more so since the Renaissance, the great masters have felt the need to synthesize in their drawings and paintings, to summarize, to abbreviate. The famous "shorthand" of Velazquez, who painted a rose with fewer brushstrokes than there were petals,

was greatly admired, and served as a lesson to the great masters of Impressionism, such as Manet, who traveled to Madrid to see and copy it first hand. And speaking of Manet: on August 10, 1907, the writer Georges Jeanniot explained in the French magazine *La Grande Revue* that he was with Manet when the latter painted *The Bar at the Folies-Bergère.* "The model," wrote Jeanniot "an attractive woman, posed behind a table filled with bottles and food. Watching Manet paint, I became aware of his masterful simplifications. Everything was abbreviated. Later Manet told me: 'In art, synthesis is a necessity and a mark of elegance. The terse man makes us think, the loquacious one bores us.'"

The watercolors of John Singer Sargent are a

1. Squinting the eyes when synthesizing.

Sargent, a master of synthesis, at one time had a few students to whom he repeated the following lesson: "Always cultivate your powers of observation. Learn to see the model through squinted eyes."

Wherever you are, if you look around you with squinted eyes, you will automatically cut out details, seeing only the large volumes, the large masses of color. Squinting, as you know, is simply looking with the eyes almost closed, maintaining a certain tension in the eyelids (see the adjoining illustration) so that the objects lose definition and appear blurry, sort of like a camera out of focus. It is good to get into the habit while painting, of occasionally looking at the model with squinted eyes. This will

317

Fig. 317—In this photograph the landscape is viewed normally. The minute details of the windows and doors can be appreciated, as well as the leaves on the plants, and the trees and shrubs in the foreground.

316

involve adopting an attitude which will undoubtedly develop your powers of observation and synthesis, essential for good watercolor painting.

318

Fig. 318—Here the same landscape is viewed as if the eyes were half closed. The merging of small forms, diffused shapes, and elimination of small details make it possible to appreciate the bodies in synthesis.

perfect example of synthesis. Sargent began studying drawing and painting at fourteen years of age, first in Florence and later in Paris, where he learned of the painter Charles Carolus-Duran. Carolus Duran taught his students to see and paint spontaneously, *au premier coup* as he put it. According to Sargent's biographers, Carolus Duran would repeat over and over again to his students the following rule, which I want to emphasize in boldface:

All that is not indispensable is prejudicial.

Synthesis in drawing and painting is expression with fewer lines, fewer brushstrokes: "corseting the details" as Ingres put it. Synthesis involves looking at the model with squinted eyes, painting with a wide brush.

Fig. 319—Velazquez, *La Infanta Margarita* (detail), The Prado, Madrid. I take the liberty of saying that I assure you that Velazquez looked at the model with his eyes half closed to achieve this "abbreviated manner," as his first master, Francesco Pacheco, called it.

319

2. Synthesizing using a large brush

This factor also has to do with your attitude, with a predisposition to summarize and interpret, difficult to obtain when painting with a fine brush, since the latter may lead you to feel an obligation to explain the small details, the intimate aspects of the shapes. Paint on rather large paper, don't paint small paintings, and paint with a large brush.

David Cox, the English watercolorist of the last century, wrote some books and treatises on watercolor painting. In one of them, according to his biographer Solly, he wrote: "I like to work with a wide brush, very damp and as full as possible of paint."

Fig. 320—If you work with small, fine brushes you will paint small, finely detailed things. A no. 3 or a no. 4 brush may be used for painting a super-realistic area, but I take the liberty of saying that super-realism is not appropriate for watercolor painting.

320

3. Synthesizing by painting rapidly

I have found, from my own experience, squinting and painting with a broad brush on a large surface an attitude that favors creativity: looking at the model—rapidly turning the head to look at the painting—the typical gesture of leaning back and stretching out the arm—making a rapid stroke with the brush—again squinting at the model—returning to the painting and adding a new color with actual fever, etc., etc. A procedure encouraging rapid painting—*alla prima,* or *au premier coup*—and carrying within it the very idea of synthesis in painting.

321

Fig. 321—John Singer Sargent, *The Bridge of Sighs,* Brooklyn Museum. In an authentic watercolor it must be possible to see the transparency of the colors, the effect of the water and the action of the brush. The synthesis of forms and colors must be obvious, as well as the spontaneity and freshness of a premeditated but rapid resolution. This is what you see in Sargent's watercolors, where the immediacy of the brushstrokes is evident.

synthesis and interpretation

322

Fig. 322—Paul Cézanne, *Still Life with Blue Vase*, Norton Timon Collection, Los Angeles. At the beginning of the century, when Cézanne was already sixty years old (he died when he was 67), he painted by suggesting rather than constructing forms and colors. These pictures are fine examples of synthesis and personal interpretation. Their success is partly due to Cézanne's ability to continue painting *his* picture for hours (Cézanne was slow), without allowing himself to be influenced by the changing forms and colors ot the model, as the hours passed.

"In art there are two paths: one is architecture and allusion; the other realities as the world shows them." This quote from the Spanish playwright Ramón M. del Valle Inclán expresses in a few words the two options an artist has: a) Painting reality, limitng oneself to the imitation of nature and copying the forms and colors just as they appear in the model; or b) Painting the architecture of Nature and the construction of the model by seeing them and interpreting them in your own way, even modifying reality. The choice between these two options leaves no room for doubt: artists have always tried to paint *their* paintings, making an effort to see the subject matter in their own way. In his "Diary," Eugène Delacroix defends the use of allusion in a discussion of the choice of subjects, saying: "You are the subject, your impressions, your emotions when confronted with Nature. You must look and see within yourself, not around yourself."

The idea of painting a painting as one sees it "from within" has been predicated by many artists, from the primitives to contemporary artists. "The primitives did not imitate Nature: Titian, Rubens and even Raphael, the classicist, interpreted much more than they copied," said Bousset. "We see Nature as something routine; the artist must see and paint it as something fantastic and fabulous," said Chagall. "The painter must set down on the canvas his internal impressions and visions," said Picasso.

To see the model in synthesis, to interpret, modify, change... that is what makes true art! In a word: we must bring the creative capacity into play.

But, what is creativity? I would say it is a new attitude *toward something we wish to change,* and this attitude crystalizes, becomes effective through imagination and fantasy. Fischer analyzed creative fantasy in his work *Art and Coexistence* and arrived at the conclusion that creativity depends on the *capacity to represent* and

323

the *capacity to combine*. In applying Fischer's theories to artistic interpretation we may say that: a) From the moment the artist analyzes the artistic possibilities of the model he recalls representations of other images he has seen and recorded because of their impact, beauty, and personal style. For instance the colors used by Van Gogh, Cézanne's forms, atmospheric effects seen in the past, chromatic harmonies recalled from a film, etc.

Recalling these images, the artist dreams, fantasizes, modifies, and changes. And b) The capacity to represent an idea different from that offered by the reality of the model causes this reality to give way to the subject that the artist "sees" with his inner eye. From there on, the artist combines what he is seeing with what he sees in it, discovering combinations of reality and memory studying new possibilities... and believing.

All very abstract, perhaps, but here are three concrete techniques for interpreting:

Augment: *make real, exaggerate, intensify*
Reduce: *decolor, soften,*
Suppress: *eliminate, cover, nullify*

Still, these and other theoretical and practical concepts are useless if, as Bonnard puts it: "The initial idea for the painting tends to evaporate when the appearance of the real model, sadly, invades and dominates the mind of the painter." Cézanne was one of the few artists who knew how to resist the seduction of the model's real appearance.

"I have a firm idea of what I plan to do with the subject matter, and I only accept from Nature what is in keeping with my ideas, my forms and my colors, according to my initial conception of the work."

This isn't exactly a magic formula, but it is the only one I know for synthesizing in painting, and for interpreting the model *according to one's own personal conception.*

Fig. 323—Julio Quesada, *Tierras de Sigüenza*, private collection. The Spanish artist, Quesada, is known to be a master of synthesis and interpretation, but it is necessary to see his work to appreciate the intelligent abstraction of forms and colors achieved with just a few colors and brush strokes. He represents figurative reality magnificently, and shows complete mastery of the watercolor technique.

thumbnail sketches

Thumbnail sketches

Take an ordinary, medium-grain 20×15 cm
$(6" \times 8")$ drawing pad and a 2B lead pencil, or
black felt tip pen or ballpoint, and go today,
tomorrow, or as soon as possible, to a place
where you can make thumbnail sketches of
the people passing by, children playing, cou-
ples talking, sitting down, drinking a refresh-
ment. If you've already done this, or are doing
it, fine, skip the following paragraphs. But if
you still haven't experienced thumbnail sketching, live from Nature, don't delay, don't lose
the opportunity. "How wonderful," said Picasso to his friend Genevieve, "that a simple
stroke can represent a living being, and not
simply his appearance, but what he really is!"
All professional artists make thumbnail sketches. A short while ago, I was in Lisbon and
made a few rough drafts while wandering the
streets of the neighborhood of Alfama. Now I
will be able to convert these drawings into
paintings. "What about the camera?" you might
ask. "Why not paint from photographs taken
of the same model?" Well, it just isn't the
same. I take photos to serve as documentation
and to remember. But an artist's sketches are
better than photographs, because you and I

324 A

Figs. 324 A and B—On the right
we see a rough lead pencil
sketch of a street in the Alfama
quarter, in Lisbon. Above is a
photograph of the same street
used as background documentation for the sketch. Compare
the two images, noting in the
rough sketch the variations the
artist has made interpreting the
subject.

324 B

Fig. 325—Eugène Delacroix,
from *Album Sketches of Morocco*, Louvre, Paris. This is the
famous "Diary" in which Delacroix made watercolor sketches
and entered written notes
concerning places and people, during his trip to North
Africa in 1832. This journey and
the documentation recorded in
the Diary on Arab themes, is
reflected in many of his fine
paintings.

325

can synthesize. We can interpret, augment, reduce, supress, remember and a camera cannot.

Making thumbnail sketches is useful in many ways. "Making sketches is like sowing seeds, in order to harvest paintings later on," wrote Van Gogh to his brother Theo. In 1832, Delacroix traveled to North Africa carrying a diary in which he recorded with brief notes and watercolor sketches, the architecture, native dress, sky colors, trees, and land of the places he visited. This was for him, a tremendously rich resource of subject matter, from which he drew a fantastic series of paintings about the daily lives of the Arab and Jewish communities.

I repeat: making thumbnail sketches is useful. There are drawing fairs everywhere, sometimes set up outside, where drawings and sketches are sold, and there are editors looking for sketches to publish in books of poetry, instructional books, and so on.

But most of all, sketching is useful because it constitutes a dynamic exercise which renews and affirms the capacity to draw. Furthermore,

drawing is often imperative in watercolor painting. When the subject is a cityscape, for example, and it is necessary to include some people in the work. One must always have the training and capabilities to draw and paint easily, and to be able to include figures which will add to the reality of the subject.

Fig. 326—Making rough sketches of people walking, chatting, relaxing, is essential in order to "keep in form" and draw and paint human figures without difficulty, whenever you decide to do a watercolor.

326

Fig. 327—In order to make my outdoor rough sketches more complete and serviceable, I paint in some of the figures when I get back to the studio, and then file them away as background for future paintings.

327

thumbnail sketches

328

329

Figs. 328, 329, and 330—Guillem Fresquet goes almost every day to a public park to make rough sketches. Some he paints on the spot, while others he paints in the studio using the rough pencil sketches as his basis. The original rough sketches measure approximately half the size of the reproductions, which is why, in some cases, Fresquet gives them to his dealer to sell as small paintings.

Fig. 331—The late painter and friend of mine, Federico Lloveras, made many rough sketches, exhibiting his extraordinary skill, and unbounded capacity for work. A rough skecth such as this took no more than twenty minutes for Lloveras.

331

watercolor painting in practice

the human figure

To discuss drawing the human figure would require an entire book in itself (in fact, I have written such a book, entitled: *How to Draw the Human Figure*). All the same, this book wouldn't be complete without a discussion of the human figure as painted in watercolors. So let us touch upon the principal points here: One of the major difficulties in drawing or painting the human figure is the problem of dimensions and proportions. Fortunately for us, the sculptors of ancient Grece, and more particularly Praxíteles formulated an idea of beauty for men and women: a canon of eight heads high by two heads wide. See fig. 333, for the comparative canons of men and women. Observe the following differences in proportion between the two sexes:

a) Women have proportionally narrower shoulders

b) Their breasts and nipples are somewhat lower

c) Their waists are somewhat narrower

d) Their bellybuttons are slightly lower

e) Their hips are proportionally wider

f) Seen from the side, the buttocks extend beyond the vertical plane drawn from the shoulderblades to the calves.

333

In order to draw or paint the human figure, it is necessary to know artistic anatomy, or as Ingres put it: "In order to express the surface of the human body, one must first understand the interior structure." Structure and movement may be studied using a jointed wooden doll, and molding may be understood by looking at the plaster casts of classic sculptures. But of course, neither these nor any other means of working will compare to the truth and quality of a human model, nude or dressed. Here the artist will find, as in no other subject matter, the opportunity to express his artistic capacities.

Fig. 333—This illustration shows the *norm* or ideal proportions for the human body, established as eight heads high by two wide. Apart from the fact that the woman is shorter, proportionally, compare the basic differences which distinguish the two sexes.

Fig. 334—The habitual study of the human body by drawing and painting from life—apart from the fact that it represents the greatest artistic merit—is essential, in order, for example, to paint a human being when clothed. Leonardo da Vinci said in this respect: "Clothing must not appear to be uninhabited. There must never be a heap of cloth or gown without support."

334

35

336

337

The clothed figure in watercolor

Fig. 335—I begin with a line drawing, and then give a first coat to the dress, taking care to leave the folds blank, working the tonal variations from light to dark.

Fig. 336—I paint the face, arms, and feet with a flesh color, but do not put in the features yet. I give a first coat to the hair and then rapidly construct the background with a first coat of patchy ochre and a scond darker coat made of Prussian blue, dark sienna, vermillion, carmine, and green.

Fig. 337—Now I can work with greater safety on the coloring of the dancing figure, her shoes, the floor...

Fig. 338—... leaving for last the features of the face, the shadow cast on the ground, and the final touches. For the darkest shadows in the dress I use Prussian blue, for the lightest, cobalt blue mixed with carmine, dark sienna and ochre. I have painted with medium-grain Arches paper in a block of a size almost twice this reproduction, using tube watercolor and sable brushes sizes 6, 12, and 14.

338

the human figure

Portraits

Painting the human head requires constant practice sketching and drawing. It is a specialty. But there is also a *canon* of ideal proportions which facilitates construction and drawing. See the adjoining study of this *canon* and notice its usefulness when you begin to draw a portrait. You will notice, for example: in all faces, the distance between the eyes is equal to the width of another eye; the location and height of the top of the ears coincides with the eyebrows; the bottom of the ears lines up with the point of the nose, etc.

A good portrait should be an exact likeness, but should also be a work of art unto itself. The resemblance depends on the features of the physiognomy, and this, according to Ingres, "always offers a caricature." This same great painter offered the following practical advice to his students.

— The body should not follow the movement of the head.
— Before beginning, chat with the model so as to get to know him/her better.
— The eyes must be drawn as if they had no importance.
— Avoid an excess of reflections.

Fig. 342—I draw a great many heads making rough sketches from live subjects, copying from magazines, television—a very entertaining experience. I have drawn a great many heads in order to be able, afterwards, to draw and paint good portraits.

342

339

A   B   C   D

a
b
c
d
e
f
g

340   341

Canon for the human head

In fig. 340 and 341 you can see two male heads, one front view and one profile. Both are drawn according to the *canon* or ideal dimensions and proportions for the human head.

Figure 339 shows the process to follow for drawing a front view of the human head according to the *canon*. Observe in A and B that the rectangle which encloses the human head is shown as three and a half units high (A), and two and a half units wide (B). Notice, finally, that in the front view shown in fig. 340, the eyes divide the height exactly in half and the nose symmetrically divides the width. In order to draw a human head or portrait, the basic lines which you should recall are letters a, b, c, d (center), e, f, and g.

343

344

345

346

347

Painting a Portrait in Watercolor

Fig. 343—I draw the subject using the *norm* (A) as reference, after I make the golden gleam of the spectacles (C) by reserving this spot with masking fluid.

Fig. 344—First I paint a general cream-colored wash, leaving blanks on the right hand side.

Fig. 345—I paint the bright and dark colors of the face without going into detail. I tone down this dark color with the brighter colors of the forehead, nose, chin using a flesh color made of ochre, vermillion, just a touch of prussian blue... carmine.

Fig. 346—While wet, I merge the dark color of the face with the color of the background. I give a first coat and some shaping to the hair, eyebrows, and moustache. I sketch the mouth, and suggest the colors of the eyes. I finish by painting the shirt.

Fig. 347—Final work: To finish the hair, I remove the masking fluid and paint in the spectacles with siennas, ochres and yellows. I paint the ears, the moustache, the mouth, and while still wet I draw the eyebrow and eye on the side of the face in shade... and leave it.

the human figure

The Nude

A good watercolor reflects the unworried, spontaneous, creative freedom of the artist. These qualities are difficult to attain in a painting of a nude done in watercolors because usually when one is painting one worries, "should I leave it like this? should I go on? is this finish sufficient?" and this excess of fear and premeditation shows up in the painting. What can we do about this? Practice sketching; then approach the painting as if it were one more sketch. Because a sketch is the maximum expression of artistic learning, a sort of miracle born of an unforeseen adventure, of "totally without worry; with spontaneity and absolute liberty."

Always draw and paint your sketches using a model—a man or woman, friend or professional—who will pose for a couple of hours. I would suggest using a professional, someone with a natural gift for posing. Read the art magazines and look into the possibility of getting together a group of two or three artists —no more—to work together and save money. Then plan each session, thinking up five or ten-minute poses, for rapid sketches, and one-hour poses for more detailed studies.

348

349

350

Figs. 348, 349, 350—While learning to draw and paint nudes, it is best to work with a professional model who has experience, knows the classical positions and can take up these positions naturally and with artistic knowledge. This professional model, posing in my studio, appears to be illuminated with daylight from the side, coming from a single opening, a broad glass window.

351

Figs. 351, 352—Every day Gaspar Romero goes to an art school where there is a nude session and draws and paints rough sketches like these. "It is the best kind of practice to keep in form" the artist assures me.

352

353

354

355

Gaspar Romero paints the Nude in Watercolor.

Fig. 353—Romero first sketches the model with very light lines, making a sort of initial framework. From this with increasingly more intense lines, he constructs the final drawing. He almost never uses an eraser.

356

357

Fig. 354. The artist painting with a gouache of a light flesh colour that he extendes all over the body. Next he applies a dry brush to absorb colour, "open" spaces and work over the modelling. The artist also uses a piece of blotting paper that he keeps next to his left hand. He quickly paints the hair with ultramarine blue and sepia.

Fig. 355. He goes over the body with a stronger flesh colour containing a little cobalt blue. With this colour and a dry brush to absorb extra water now and then he works over the modelling. He uses Hoocker green to paint the background next to the head, burnt umber, Hoocker green and car-

mine for the piece of furniture and cobalt blue for the upholstered seat.

Fig. 356 and 357. Always using just a number 12 brush, extending the flesh colour that now has slight traces of carmine and blue, and absorbing now and the either with a piece of blotting paper or a dry brush, Gaspar Romero reaches the final stage in deep concentration and feverish activity, modelling and finishing parts of the body, face features and so on. He stops when he signs. He has taken 40 minutes all in all.

painting skies and clouds

In the English countryside, near Suffolk, at 9:00 a.m. on September 15, 1830, the sky was clear. At about 11:00 a strong wind came up out of the west which rapidly filled the sky with a partial covering of storm clouds.

John Constable was there, painting the sky and clouds in watercolors (fig. 358). On the back of this watercolor, Constable made a note of the place, day, and hour that these clouds appeared in the sky.

The sky has drawn the attention of many artists. Constable said: "The sky is the source of Nature's light; it rules the entire landscape." Alfred Sisley, the French Impressionist painter, considered the sky to be a very important part of a painting: "I always begin with the sky; the sky is not a simple backwash, a shiny abyss. The sky is brother to the plain, and is composed of planes just like the earth. It forms a part of the general rhythm of the painting."

Of course the sky is important and worth studying.

There are skies and skies: clear, smooth skies which may be easily finished with a simple wash, remembering only to *lighten the color in the lowest part of the horizon*. There are clear skies with soft curlicues of clouds which look like cotton, also easily finished by absorbing paint and "opening-up" the white of the clouds with a clean damp brush and some absorbent paper tissues. In very wide skies in large watercolors, the white of these clouds may also be opened up with a sponge.

But then there are skies like those Constable painted, or skies with big, full-bodied cumulus clouds; with brilliant lights and soft shadows, sometimes combined with stormy, dark gray clouds... and these skies aren't so easy. All the same, they are perfectly possible. There are, in my opinion, three basic factors necessary to paint one of these skies:

1. *Construction.* A sky with concrete clouds cannot be improvised, and shouldn't be painted without first preparing a well constructed line drawing which shows where and how each shape begins and ends: a calculated drawing, unhurried but without pauses.

2. *Volume and color.* Carefully study the location of the sun and the direction of the light, observing, that the sky-blue color, whether

359

Fig. 358—John Constable — *Study of Clouds above a Broad Landscape Between 11 and 12 in the Morning — September 15, 1830 — Wind from the West,* Victoria and Albert Museum, London. Constable painted various watercolors of clouds on the backs of which he recorded the type of wind and the date and time when they were painted. His consistent interest in, and study of nature was translated into painting the best English landscapes of his time.

Fig. 359, 360—To begin, it is good to make rough sketches, life studies, and studies of skies and clouds, using a lead pencil on white paper. In addition, draw skies and clouds with a carbon pencil stump, and white chalk on colored paper, studying the varying shades and volumes.

360

Fig. 363—I paint the top of the clouds with different shades of gray, basically ultramarine and dark Sienna, but mixing in carmine, ochre, cobalt blue...

362

Fig. 364—I intensify some areas, particularly the bottom and darkest part of the clouds. I finish the clouds and outline the color of the landscape; I moisten the sky at the horizon and working wet-in-wet, I paint the blue hill in the background and outline the two trees in bright green.

Watercolor study of sky with clouds.

Fig. 361—A rapid but confident drawing—unfinished drawings, badly done, are of no use for our purposes.

Fig. 362—I begin with the blue of the sky—Prussian blue, ultra-marine, and just a suggestion of ochre—outlining the block of clouds and leaving a number of blank areas within. Then I fuse the cloud mass together with a general blue, creating only slight variations of tone and color. On the fringe, where the sky joins the horizon, I lighten the blue with water and add just a touch of yellow.

Fig. 365—I continue with the landscape which suggests a dominant warm yellow-ochre, but including carmine, bright green, purples, and blues. To finish, I paint a very bright glaze of ochre and yellow on the clouds to give a warm tone, which blends with the dominant quality of the landscape.

365

painting skies and clouds

dark or light, outlines the luminous white of the clouds and acts as a background. We should notice that often the gray colors of the shadows in the clouds are lighter than the blue sky of the background, and we must constantly compare the *values* of these grays and see the blue, pink, and golden tendencies of these shadow grays, so that the clouds will finally become real.

3. *Technique.* Finally, we should be aware of the watercolor techniques required in each instance, previously reserving whites, outlining illuminated parts, with the sky as the background, attaining the forms of the model, modeling with tones acheived with the brush and absorbent paper, daubing here, adding there, working and painting with real drive—and with real urgency, because the clouds literally fly away!—without losing sight of the model, *without losing the white highlights* which define the basic characteristics of clouds.

"The sky comes first," said Sisley, and all professional watercolor artists begin with the sky when painting landscapes. And they do it absolutely without worry, joyfully and with guile, as though making a bet with themselves: "I'll bet I can! I can paint this cloudy sky with a few brushstrokes and a few dabs of absorbent paper." And they do it! They succeed! It is a daily game: to start with the sky without thinking, without bother, without the fearful conciousness of an amateur. "And, if it doesn't come out, I remarked to one of my students, leave it and start again."
Agreed?

Fig. 366—In this high mountain landscape, I have painted a classical sky with clouds on a luminous day where the gray shadows of the clouds are brighter than the blue of the sky. The intensification of lights and shadows, without sliding into the latter, is very important.

Fig. 367—Federico Lloveras *Palacio Real (Madrid),* private collection. Here, an overcast sky is painted wet-in-wet with applications of grays, perfectly controled by the artist which allow the sky to have a very important role, conditioning the color of the urban landscape which he has resolved with a range of pale color.

Fig. 368 1— Ceferino Olivé, *Arenales (Riudoms),* private collection. Ceferino Olivé painted this dramatic landscape with a range of warm colors, working with coarse brushes in long and broad strokes, blending, absorbing, always "straight off", giving it everything, staking everything.

Sky and clouds with a special range of color

Fig. 369—Having finished the sketch, I lay in a uniform wash of ochre made to look dirty with just a whisper of blue and dark sienna, reserving white areas for the houses of the town, to be painted later.

369

370

371

372

373

Fig. 370—Once the background is dry, I paint over it using the same color, made darker with more sienna, blending to bring out parts of the clouds. With different Siennas I paint the houses and some areas of the ground.

Fig. 371—Now I paint the color of the sky using ultramarine, carmine and ochre, brightening the color on reaching the horizon. I continue with the houses, the shadows, and the roofs.

Fig. 372—I finish the sky with a last wet application in the bottom areas of the clouds. I finish the sky and complete the plots of land and roads of the town.

Fig. 373—For the finishing touches I use a fine ball point pen with which I draw a number of the lines of the houses, the roofs, some furrows in the ground, some figures, etc.

painting trees

The first thing to remember when painting trees is that they have a structure, a skeleton; they are trunks and branches with a covering, a clothing made of leaves. The skeleton is important. If you draw or sketch trees without leaves, in the winter, with only the scaffolding of the bare branches, not only will you have a great time, but you will also rapidly learn to paint trees. And if you afterwards dedicate a good deal of time to drawing trees, bushes, and thickets, as Van Gogh did continuously, you will learn to paint trees placed far in the distance, or set up close in the foreground.

There are no tricks or secrets, only careful observation and understanding: branch groups extend from the trunk, leaves form clusters which determine the effects of light and shadow on the colors and forms of the tree. The combinations of trunks, branches, and leaves are sometimes broken up, leaving spaces through which we see the light of the sky, illuminating their dark silhouettes. And we must paint them as they really are: with blues, yellows, and ochres (trees have a lot of green-ochre color) in the top part, and with more green than yellow, more blue than ochre in the lower part, which is in shade and reflect the color and light of the earth. Tree trunks have the forms of small spheres or cylinders which are illuminated from above. When they appear alone or grouped together in the distance, they are always darker than the meadows and fields around them.

The next time you are in the country, look at them... and paint them.

Figs. 374, 375—Making good sketches and drawings of trees without leaves is good exercise for drawing them with greater familiarity.

Fig. 376—Here are several trees seen in the middle distance; thus their shapes and colors have been resolved using synthesis.

Fig. 377—A step-by-step demonstration of painting a tree seen in the middle distance, using only a few strokes to suggest form and color.

378

379

380

381

382

Painting a landscape with trees.

Fig. 378—Drawing trees in the foreground of the drawing, like drawing clouds, is not something you can half do, unless you have extraordnary experience.

Fig. 379—First, applications of uniform color in diluted washes, with certain shades calculated to enrich the color.

Fig. 380—I resolve the sky, the clouds, and the background of gray and blue mountains using the wet-in-wet technique.

Fig. 381—I paint the tree in the foreground, resolving the shape and color of the groupings of leaves, painting at the top with greens tending to ochre, and at the bottom with greens which have a blue tint. I paint the trunk and the branches of the tree, as well as the shade it casts— without completing it. I resolve the fragment of a house which appears on the left-hand side, as well as the shade it casts. I intensify the foreground colors, and to the fields in the middle distance, I add a pink and an ochre green.

Fig. 382—I finish the cast shadow in the foreground by the tree, I give a first application, both drawing and painting the tress and bushes in the meadow in the middle, and I paint a number of dark highlights which enrich the foreground.

Fig. 383—I finish the foreground and background trees, intensify a number of colors and add some finishing touches.

383

painting a landscape in watercolors

In these pages we begin a series of exercises for watercolor painting in which, step by step, you will be able to study the resolution of several paintings painted by several artists.

The first of these watercolors was created by the renowned artist Ceferino Olivé, who has been awarded several national and international prizes, for his watercolors, now found in museums and private collections in France, England, Germany, the United States, Japan Italy and elsewhere.

Ceferino Olivé is a professional veteran, a partisan of pure watercolor without stains, without liquid glue or wax pencil. He doesn't wet the paper, nor does he mount it with glued paper strips (paper tape) in order to tighten it. He uses, exclusively, thick brushes made out of ox hair, of such high numbers as 12, 18, 24 and 30, each with a special handle, as long as that of an oil brush (30 cm).

He paints with tube watercolor; using a metal palette, like the one reproduced in page 63, and works with a three legged atelier's easel. He paints with the paper in an almost vertical position.

A very personal technique

All watercolor professionals that I know of, including myself, use absorbent papers, raw cotton, a cotton rag, or a sponge, in order to discharge or absorb liquid, color, or the water from the brush. Ceferino Olivé is different. Instead of a water jar he uses a water bucket like one used for mopping floors. He places the water bucket beside him, next to his chair. In order to wring moisture out of the brush,

384

Fig. 384—Ceferino Olivé, a famous watercolor veteran with innumerable prizes and with works in museums and collections throughout the world, is an example of commonsense, sobriety and simplicity, which is why a look at his studio is instructive for us. "All my life I have painted in the open air," he tells me, I have painted in almost all the cities of Europe and I have always done it with the same equipment: an easel to hold the board with the paper, a seat, and a case in which I carry the colors and utensils for painting. I never paint in the studio, and if sometimes I have to do it, then I prefer to work under exactly the same conditions as when I paint in the open air." And so it is that in one of his studios, apart from a large table and a bookcase filled with books, there is no other equipment other than an easel set at a 45° angle, and a small low table. It is within this very place that we see him signing a painting.

385

Fig. 385—Ceferino Olivé. *Smokey Tunnel*, private collection. Here is a good example of the style of Ceferino Olivé, in its composition, harmony of color, technique, and drawing or construction, all of which are truly enviable.

he shakes his arms with the brush on his hand, as if he were whipping, as if sprinkling, spattering water on the floor which he covers with wrapping paper to avoid wetting and dirtying it. It is to be noted, as well, the way in which he holds the brush very high up, with the handle inside the hand.

As we shall see as we follow the development of his painting, Ceferino Olivé is everywhere when he paints: looking at everything at once, painting sometimes here, sometimes there, indeed everywhere at once, and in this way the painting advances progressively toward its final stage.

First stage: the drawing (Fig. 388)

Ceferino Olivé draws with a no. 2 regular pencil. He keeps at hand a very soft kneaded eraser which is a dark gray color though he practically never uses it. He uses fine-grain paper which he secures to the drawing board with four metal clips. This watercolor is 70 × 50 cm. He draws with the pencil stick inside his hand, rapidly, with very few lines, rapidly sketching the basic forms of the model without

bothering with small details. What he does is to locate the basic forms: the tower in the background, the tiled roofs of the houses, the hardly indicated profiles of the trees, the thickest tree trunks.

"It's all done", he says. "There's nothing missing." And he gets the palette, fills it with colors, and starts painting.

Second stage: trying out the color (Fig. 389)

Watching Ceferino Olivé paint is a true spec-

Fig. 386—Observe this special manner of holding the very end of the brush handle which, according to Olivé, obliges him to paint at a distance, free, without ever falling into the fatal pitfall of discribing small details.

Fig. 387—Ceferino Olivé, *Reflections (Castellón,* private collection). Another example of the personal technique of Ceferino Olivé, obvious proof of his extraordinary facility to construct and paint in a few strokes, explaining the subject with a language which is sober, correct, and at once different and brilliant.

painting a landscape in watercolors

tacle. In the sky, for instance: he charges brush no. 24 with ultramarine blue, he dirties it with a bit of Payne's gray and paints with wide strokes, from right to left, leaving white spaces, and with unexpected rapidity. I would dare say with fever, he plunges the brush in the water bucket, rinses it, discharges the excess water, whipping and sprinkling, and within a fraction of a second he is back in the sky, diluting and degrading the blue with the white of the paper, in a technique that looks as if it were wet, because of the perfect blending of some watercolors with others. And he leaves it like this with the enviable certainty that "he has solved the blue color of the sky." Now, even faster—if that is possible—as if the success of the painting depended on it, he mixes an orange and applies it to the tower and to the houses in the background, modifying it, as he goes along, with some green, gray, blue, and vermillion strokes; and in a few seconds he covers the white of the paper.

Third stage: determining the form (Fig. 390)
One should wait a few minutes for the previous stage to dry. In the meantime, Ceferino Olivé looks attentively at the sky, making faces while he holds the brush in his hand. "The sky is the roof," he says. he observes the towers, the houses...
Suddenly, he mixes a light gray using ultramarine blue, sienna, and a little gray, and dilutes it with water. With this light gray, he paints the whites that remain in the sky. He rinses, whips, sprinkles. He blends the grays, and... the clouds make their appearance! Now he lightens this gray with water, adds a bit more sienna, and solves the color of the sky at the horizon. The sky, "the roof" is done. This is how the painting will remain.
Ceferino Olivé now mixes up a sienna-carmine-vermillion color, and with varied but certain strokes, solves the shadows of the houses, grass, and bushes in the foreground. He then changes the colors and paints the mountains in the backgrund, the green of a tree, and the grass at the edge of the foreground. With this he has resolved the forms and their volume. It reminds me of the words of Edouard Manet, who in his letter to the young G. Heannot, said: "It is in the forms that I look for the most intense light and the deepest shadow; everything else is given to me in the bargain."

Fourth stage: The "maestro's phase" (Fig. 391)
Ceferino Olivé calls this phase the "master

Fig. 388—A drawing, barely indicated with a no. 2 pencil, already places and proportions the forms and elements of the subject. A fact, which will become more obvious in the following figures, is that Olivé draws as he paints.

Fig. 389—Observe in this and the subsequent stages how Olivé does not paint isolated parts or areas of the picture, but paints, draws, and shapes "everything all at once, pushing ahead with the whole picture at the same time," so that he could stop painting halfway through and he would already have done a painting.

390

Fig. 390—Ceferino Olivé is a classicist; In a previous stage he colored the paper. On reaching this, the second stage, he painted the most important shadows of the subject, as if he were following the advice of Corot who said: "First the values; second the shadows."

cloak." "After this phase," he explains, "it's only a question of embroidering, that is to say, of detailing, rectifying some forms, creating some contrasts; but the painting is finished for all practical purposes." Ceferino Olivé washes the palette with water, using one of his thickest brushes. He then intensifies the color of the tile roofs of the houses with a series of vertical or diagonal lines, many of which blend in a regular watercolor area. He now paints the thickest of the tree trunks on the left with a warm gray; he applies a dirty green to the

foreground right and to the trees on the left, with wide and daring strokes, intensifying and clarifying as he goes along, opening up whites by scratching with the back of his thumb nail or the nail of his baby finger, to expose strokes of light color. To the green of the trees he adds a light red-ochre on the left hand side, always with the formula of first applying the brush filled with color, and next degrading the intense paint by means of diluting with water. At last, he leaves the piece alone.

painting a landscape in watercolors

Fig. 391—According to Ceferino Olivé this is "the master stage or phase of the painting." When this stage is finished the painting is already right regarding composition, form and color. There remain only the possibilities, of enriching the color, of creating greater contrasts...

391

Fig. 392—In fact, between the painting of the previous illustration, fig. 390, and these two more advanced stages, there has been a general enrichment both of forms and details, contrast, and color. But the intellectual effort, the uncertainty and anguish of the painting which is taking shape, is already passed. What follows now is, an *entertainment*, a true festival in which the artist feels himself carried away by the color and the contrast.

392

393

Fifth stage: almost finished (Fig. 392)

He cleans the palette again before he paints the vertical and diagonal strokes from the tile roofs, always with that loose air which, in the long run, promotes the feeling of lively, vibrant color. He finally fills the brush with a dark, earthy color with which he decidedly resolves the foreground contrasts, placing with capricious strokes the stains on the trees on the left, clarifying some contours, as his brush "walks" around the painting, working here and there, everywhere—except in the sky.

Sixth and last phase: final touches (Fig. 393)

Little remains to be done. Almost everything is finished... but the artist, after a long pause, after having looked alternately from the painting to the model, after cleaning the palette and smoking a cigarette, begins making small last minute changes. He finishes the trees on the left, reinforces the hills in the background, insists on the tile roof of the house on the left, and clarifies the bushes in the right foreground, and the reflection of the small stream. After a long silence, during which he looks ecstatically at the painting, Ceferino Olivé says: "It's done. Let's leave it."

Fig. 393—In this last stage Ceferino Olivé has done very little; he has spent a lot of time looking, observing... it is the moment of considering and reconsidering, and even of getting up and taking a walk, of having a cup of coffee, before returning with the mind cleared to either continue or to *leave it to time:* "Yes, to leave it to time is important," Olivé emphasizes.

painting a sea port in watercolors

Guillermo Fresquet, the second guest artist who is going to paint a watercolor for us, chooses a theme on the sea port. His experience as a watercolor painter places him among the top artists of Spain; his paintings have been awarded in numerous contests and his extraordinary capacity as a draftsman and painter allows him to paint for us in his studio, using some notes and sketches drawn in the open air as his model.

Fresquet has created this watercolor from some notes taken in Barcelona port, and has added the old carriages pulled by horses that used to meander around the freight piers of twenty or thirty years ago.

Fresquet uses medium-grain paper, about 350 grams. He paints with tube watercolors and a white metal, enamel palette, with compartments in the center to hold the color. He paints with round brushes of marten hair, generally nos. 9, 12, 14, 18 and 22; he also uses the flat brush, no. 16, for backgrounds and wide gray hues. Occasionally he uses a round brush no. 14 and another no. 6 to execute lines and thin strokes. He works with two plastic flasks of water: one for the water with which he paints, and the other to clean his brush. He paints on a common table with a drawing board slanted about 30 degrees, in a small studio, as can be seen here.

First stage: the drawing (Fig. 394)
Fresquet draws with an HB pencil and rarely uses his eraser. He draws with an amazing certainty, defining the forms with a few strokes, eliminating shading, drawing figures, carriages, and animals from memory and knowledge.

Second stage: general background tones (Fig. 395)
Fresquet begins with the background. First the sky is painted using a flat brush no. 16. He starts by painting in the light orange-yellow color in the upper sections, and immediately following while the orange is still wet, he lays in the overall gray of the sky. The layers become mixed and diluted, producing the illusion of the sun on a half misty morning. He continues with the gray on both sides and toward the lower part. He may first discharge a little of the gray by wringing the brush with a cotton rag. He adds a generous rose tone to the horizon, reserving a brief thin strip of white paper for the sea. With a warm color he paints the reflection of the sky on the water and land, again reserving a few strips of white paper that

Fig. 394—As can be seen in this illustration, Guillermo Fresquet resolves the drawing of his watercolor with considerable detail and perfection.

Fig. 395—Note that the watercolor with which Fresquet paints the sky extends over the whole picture; only the strip of sea and the pools of water in the foreground have been reserved. While the sky was still wet, Fresquet used a fine brush to "open up" the diffused white smoke of the boat in the foreground and the nebulous white in the left-hand background.

Fig. 396—In Fresquet's water-colors the first application is the one that counts; there is almost never a second or third application. Studying the development of this watercolor, in the phases described on the following pages, you will see that the forms and colors of this second stage are already definitive, and will appear as they are here in the finished picture.

396

will later serve to represent water puddles. Before leaving the first stage, Fresquet wets certain areas and absorbs some of the color into his brush; he diffuses the intensity of the color in the areas which correspond to the smoke billowing out of the ships.

Third stage: resolution of the basic forms (Fig. 396)

Fresquet works slowly but without pauses. His extraordinary experience as a watercolor art-ist, and his notable capacity as a draftsman, allow him to resolve the painting step by step, thinking ahead which parts are definitely solved, which forms are on hold, and what areas he will have to elaborate on later, in order to finish the painting. In this third phase he paints the middle ground, super-imposed on the general tone of the sky, always maintain-ing a perfectly harmonized color range. Ob-serve the slight differences in contrast be-tween foreground and background, especially on the right side of the painting, where he begins to suggest atmosphere and depth.

397

Fig. 397—The artist Guillermo Fresquet working in his studio. Observe that the board on which he paints in the studio appears to be very steeply in-clined, some 20° to 25°, and is supported in a very rudimen-tary manner. What is more, the studio is a very small room.

painting a sea port in watercolors

Fig. 398—So far, Fresquet has painted this watercolor *in planes,* that is to say, resolving the background first (fig. 396), and now superimposing a nearer plane as on the house curtains of a stage.

398

Fig. 399—Fresquet continues with the idea of working *in planes,* working in specific areas, contrasting and accentuating the carriages in the foreground to bring them nearer.

399

400

Fig. 400—At this point compare the various stages with the finished painting; study the shades used in the range of pale colors, the resolution of the planes, creating the idea of a graduated distance and atmosphere; note the contrast between tones and how they are accentuated in the nearest forms; Notice the synthesis of forms and colors, particularly obvious in the figures and carriages; and, finally, enjoy Fresquet's easy and spontaneous way of painting a watercolor.

Fourth stage: emphasizing the depth (Fig. 398)
In this fourth stage Fresquet defines distances with color. He intensifies some colors in the middle ground formed by the crane and the ship on the right, but leaves the more distant forms in light gray, and in the more sketchy drawing of the last stage. With more color and detail he defines the horse and carriage in the foreground, but leaves the activity in the distance, in a penumbra of shapes and colors. The color range is kept to sepia, ultramarine blue, Payne's gray, green... painting loosely, with plenty of water.

Fifth and last stage: final touches (Fig. 399/400)
We have divided the final stage into two steps in order to understand the order of these last touches applied to resolve the painting. He begins by defining the carriages and animals, in great detail, especially the figures in the foreground. He adds figures, shadows, some small shapes, the ground in the foreground, the reflections in the water puddles... and his signature.

painting a seascape in watercolors

Gaspar Romero is the author of this luminous watercolor, painted on the dock of a sailing club.

Until a short while ago, Gaspar Romero was an excellent amateur, but he recently became a professional, and has for some years been the president of the Watercolorists Congress of Catalonia, a group with more than three hundred associate members, including some of the best watercolor artists in Spain. Our guest artist has written and lectured on many occasions about watercolor painting, and is an expert in the field.

Gaspar Romero habitually paints on fine grain paper, in this case on a tablet 62 × 146 cm, made by Fabriano. He uses three brands of paint interchangeably: tube watercolors by Grumbacher or Winsor and Newton and the line of damp watercolor tablets by Schminke. His brushes are a special type featuring a mixture

of synthetic and sable hairs recently introduced by Winsor and Newton, in nos. 6, 8, 12 and 14. Explains Gaspar Romero: "These brushes with mixed hairs work well. On the other hand, those with all synthetic hair fail to hold enough

401

Fig. 401—Gaspar Romero paints with the board supported on an easel, almost vertical. "You should emphasize," he tells me, "that it is perfectly possible to paint in watercolor with the board or support almost vertical."

water, as if they reject or spit out the watercolor liquids."

Gaspar Romero uses the typical palette, with indentations in the middle and mixing trays on each side; made of metal and finished with white enamel. His studio tripod is the classical workshop tripod, but when he paints outside, he uses a tripod with three folding legs. "It is perfectly possible to paint in watercolors with the support almost vertical, changing the idea that some amateurs have, that it is necessary to work with the support in an almost horizontal position." Romero paints with only one small container of water (about one half liter), because, as he says: "It is good to paint with the water a little bit dirty because this relative dirtiness helps to create atmosphere and to harmonize the colors."

First stage: drawing (Fig. 404)

Gaspar Romero draws with an ordinary no. 2 pencil and a Pelikan G-20 plastic eraser, dark gray in color and quite soft. He draws very carefully, considering every stroke, even using the ruler for those shapes that demand it. He draws only a few lines, with no shadows. "I work slowly, paying a lot of attention to my drawing, partially because I want to avoid

403

Fig. 403—To draw a boat is relatively simple, so long as perspective is taken into consideration and is present in all the lines flowing toward the horizon.

404

Fig. 402—Gaspar Romero, *Landscape, Santa Maria de Besora*, artist's collection. A landscape of a small town in the Pyrenees, painted on a cold autumn morning, with the mist invading the background. Distance is emphasized with the paintbrush, painting the belfry and the church façade to contrast with the violet and cobalt blue background mist. Also to be noted is the interpretation of forms and colors in synthesis, particularly the white road and its environs.

Fig. 404—Gaspar Romero draws slowly and pays particular attention to construction of the theme, "partly to avoid using the eraser", he explains, "but also to paint afterward with more certainty."

painting a seascape in watercolors

using the eraser which can alter the fibres of the paper, but also so that I can paint with a surer hand afterwards."

Second stage: the background "from the top down" (Fig. 405)

"Yes, I'm going to paint this watercolor from the top down," says Gaspar Romero, "because-the sky and the pier in the background, behind the boats, make a unit that must be finished first, and everything at the same time." And that's just how he does it. Starting with the sky, using a no. 14 brush with a rounded tip, he paints large washes of weak color, first a green mixed with sienna, then a cobalt blue. He paints everything very rapidly, directing the wash to one side and then the other. Suddenly he turns the support upside down and paints with the painting upside down, still controlling the wash, and slowly building up the color in the upper part of the painting, where the sky will be later on. While he waits for this application to dry, he paints the sides of some of the boats with a very light wash, "in order to be able to play with a reserve of whites later on." He reinforces the blanks with a darker color of ultramarine and sienna in the

shed in the background and in the building on the right-hand side. Painting while still damp, he reinforces the blue and dark sienna of the base, and then uses the beveled handle of the paintbrush to rub forcefully, drawing white strokes which correspond to the masts and railings of the pier. Using sienna, he delineates the upper part of the roof of the pier with a horizontal stroke, and then moves to the right-hand side, to begin the form of the reddish boat in the shipyard.

Third stage: the boats (Fig. 406)

There isn't much to explain: Gaspar Romero finishes the forms and colors of the boats, drawing and painting barrels, boarders, cabins, small details. Afterwards he darkens the base of the pier, and before it is totally dry, he scratches with the nail of his index finger, opening the vertical lines at the base. Using a flat no. 8 brush of synthetic hair, he "opens up" the white of the parallel masts of the boats on the left-hand side, in the following manner: first he dampens the masts with water, applying the edge of the brush, going over it a few times, from top to bottom. Then he cleans the brush, and returns, softening and diluting the

Fig. 405—At this second stage, Gaspar Romero paints wet-in-wet and tries out the effect of marking white lines with the brush handle ends. Some of these lines, the gray of the sky, the grays of the background, and some dark areas are already defined and will remain like this in the finished water-color.

405

Fig. 406—Gaspar Romero has now created a major contrast obscuring the background where the boats are; he has "opened out" some vertical lines in the background (with the end of the brush), and the whites corresponding to the boat masts, damping and absorbing color with a synthetic hairbrush.

406

Fig. 407—The landing stage on the left side and also the hull appearing in the background to the right have been worked out, painted with some lack of definition so that they are situated further out. Note the care with which the artist has presented the luminous outlines of the boats and see how these colors, which were worked out in the preliminary drawing, are still defined in the painting.

407

painting a seascape in watercolors

Fig. 408—This dark wash, the reflection of the boats on the sea, was painted quickly and decisively, clarifying the boundaries of the bottom part of the picture, while deliberately leaving a number of small white areas in the interior. Most important, is that he painted wet-in-wet, diversified the color with different shades, mixing on the paper itself with ultramarine, dark sienna, carmine...

408

blue color. Finally, he drains the brush, absorbing the water and color, allowing the white to appear on the paper. He uses the same brush and technique to "open up" the white of the searchlight lamp on the top of the boat in the center.

Fourth stage: a transitional phase (Fig. 407)

The decisive moment for the painting is drawing near. Soon Gaspar Romero will have to finish the reflections of the boats in the water with a few brushstrokes. If it comes out well, fine; but if it comes out wrong... For that reason he works more slowly now, looking at the water again and again, noticing unimportant shapes and details. He works on the right side a little bit, and then the dark base of the pier. He looks again at the water and finishes the ship in the shipyard, painting the dock in the left foreground... he stops.

Fifth stage: the big risk (Fig. 408)

"You'll risk it, right?" I ask him.
"Of course, but I have to *throw myself into the water* without fear," he answers, smiling.
And so Gaspar bravely "jumps in." Using a rounded no. 24 brush, with the slightly dirty

Fig. 409—At a specific moment, before this dark area has dried, Gaspar Romero finds his lamp, lights it, and brings it close to the painting to accelerate his drawing. it is an original trick... which has its risk.

409

water he has been using all along, he dampens the zone corresponding to the reflections, with the result that since the dirty water is light gray, he can see and reserve the white forms corresponding to the actual reflections of the boats, while drawing the lower profile, the capricious shapes of the water in the foreground, etc. He follows with ultramarine blue, a little Sienna and a touch of carmine, forming a blued gray that he applies to the zone he has already dampened, working rapidly: adding color here, absorbing a little there, lightly varying the nuances.

"Nice job, Gaspar. You did it!" (Fig. 410)

Afterwards, with a flat no. 10 brush of synthetic hair, he "opens up" the sinuous whites

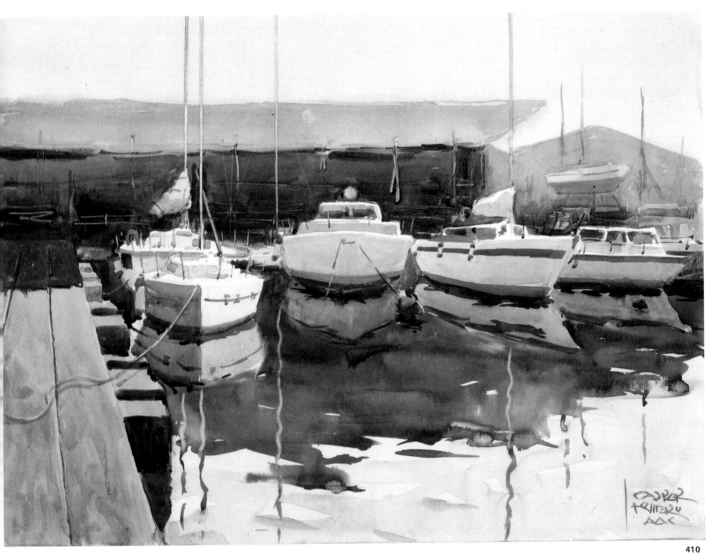

410

corresponding to the reflections of the light-colored masts, painting the reflection of the mast on the foreground white, darkening the reflection of the boat in the left foreground and... "That's it, right?" I ask. "Not yet," says Gaspar, "the reflections of the boats are too light, they look like holes, they must be darkened. Reflections are always darker than the actual color of the reflected object."

Sixth and last stage: finishing
And he does it. First he waits for the dark wash of the ocean to dry, (speeding up the drying process by holding a cigarette lighter flame up to the damp part. "It's a little bit risky, but nothing will happen... if I do it right." When it is dry he paints these nuances which conscientiously flee the uniform gray regularity. And still he paints, setting in the foreground, light color stains representing the movement of the water.
"Now it's done," he says, and signs his name.

Fig. 410—This is the final stage of the painting—but watch what the artist does: he darkens the bright reflections of the boats on the sea, ("the reflection is always darker than the color of the form which is reflected") and with water straight out of the container (and somewhat dirty), he makes a number of brushstrokes which result in a very bright gray color, on the white paper in the foreground to represent the slight undulations of the sea.

painting an illustration in watercolors

Maria Rius is a famous illustrator with children's books published in many countries. She paints watercolors with liquid, transparent colors, using the white of the paper. Although her technique is not exactly that of the "pure" watercolorist, her way of solving problems, her methods and procedures—including her tricks—I believe justify including her work in this book.

Maria Rius's palette of liquid watercolors, covers the whole color gamut—18 colors in all —and all of a specific trademark. She prefers a line of colors called "pastel" paints which reflect the gentleness and bright luminosity of pastel colors. She uses high quality fine grain paper, about 300 grams. She paints with three brushes of marten hair: nos. 8 and 10 for the overall painting, and a no. 3 for the small details. She uses two water containers, one for the first rinsing, and the other with cleaner water, for complete washing, absorbing colors, etc. Lastly, as is the case with all modern illustrators, Maria Rius uses the airbrush to fill in and resolve backdrops, blendings and graduating tones, and for large areas of uniform color. The illustration created especially for this book does not correspond to a particular story or theme. I simply requested a *creative illustration,* and Maria Rius created a free image—for once without the conditions imposed by the editor!" She has imagined an activity which everybody, children and adults, have dreamed of doing at least once: the act of flying! Congratulations Maria!

The technique

The classic watercolor demands cleanness, will countenance only limited use of erasing, prohibits dirtiness, smudgy fingerprints, or muddying of the tones which might cause alterations in color or stains. This type of care should be taken to a rigorous, antiseptic extreme for the art of illustration. The rubber eraser is forbidden; the pencil foundation drawing must be very light to avoid showing through the applied watercolor. A small drop of water or saliva on a uniform background damages the illustration; one has to work with a paper under the working hand so the palm will not dirty the work that has been done, or the white paper.

These precautions start as soon as the drawing begins. The professional illustrator never draws directly on the final piece of art. Rather, on a separate sheet of paper, she studies the composition, the pose, the attitudes and expressions

Fig. 411—(Above) The table of the illustrator Maria Rius with two water receptacles on the right-hand side, the bottles of liquid watercolor, and the porcelain dishes which the artist uses as a palette.

Fig. 412—A first projection, drawn in pencil on ordinary paper.

PAINTING WATERCOLOR WITH AN AIR BRUSH

Generally an air brush is not used for artistic watercolors, which does not mean that on certain occasions, in order to obtain certain effects such as smooth grading or blending, graded strokes, the effects of mist, etc., it might not be advisable to use it. Today in the field of illustration, the air brush is an indispensable tool. As a result of this requirement, and since under certain circumstances this knowledge may be useful to you, we thought it a good idea, while Maria Rius was producing her illustration, to explain briefly the function and technique of the airbrush.

Fig. 413—Characteristics and mechanics of the airbursh for artists. The "gun" is operated by an air compressor, which the artist controls with a pedal, leaving the hands free to control the extremely fine spray of paint forced out by the mechanism.

413

Fig. 414—Before beginning to spray the color, the artist must check it on a separate piece of paper, having first prepared the necessary quantity of color in a cup or small mug.

414

Fig. 415—With the color already prepared, one should test the gun, loading it with water to prevent possible setbacks, such as the gun being dirty, blocked, etc. Having carried out this prior check, use a coarse brush to transfer the liquid paint from the cup in which it has been prepared to the small reservoir of the air brush, filling it approximately halfway.

415

Fig. 416—Before finally painting, carry out a test on any piece of paper, making sure that there can be no splashing which on the paper and final drawing would mean an irreversible mishap.

Fig. 417—Having taken all the necessary precautions, painting can begin with the airbrush, checking the intensity of the blend or the evenness of the gray, since, if it is very dark and requires more than one application, it is necessary to wait for it to dry in order to intensify it with new applications of spray. Notice how far away from the picture Maria works while she is holding the gun and painting.

417

Fig. 418—Here Maria Rius is painting a change of shades or colors with a stencil; this remains fixed in place over the original drawing by some pieces of lead or small standard weights, typically used to make sure that the stencil is not moved by the movement of air from the air brush. In order to better understand what Maria Rius is doing here, look at the blends and change of colors in the illustration shown in fig. 423.

418

419

Fig. 419—On a small scale, these are the blended strips of color against a background of color, produced by the air brush and a stencil which Maria Rius moved gradually upwards. The resolution of this series of blended strips or boundaries can be seen more clearly on the following pages.

420

Fig. 420—The air brush, with the outlet pipe suitably sealed, can draw fine shades and strokes of blended colors like those reproduced here.

painting an illustration in watercolors

421

422

Figs. 421, 422—After having produced several pencil studies, Maria Rius drew these sea-gulls and this figure which could already be used for a finished illustration.

Fig. 423—Here is the background painted with an air brush on which, if you look closely, it is possible to see the line drawing of the sea-gulls and the figure of the flying child.

Observe that this background has been reserved with adhesive tape, in order to provide a frame or white margin around the illustration.

423

of the figures and animals, all the important elements. These studies are usually done in pencil, on visualizing or tracing paper, both of which are nearly transparent. In this way, if any one of these sketches turns out to be perfect, it may be transferred by tracing it onto the definitive drawing. The tracing is usually done by blackening the back of the tracing paper which has the selected drawing. This blackening, made with pencil, works as carbon paper. However, this can be messy and cause carbon to come off on the good paper. The best method of transferring is to use a light box with the tracing paper and drawing paper on top. Maria Rius drew several studies of sea-gulls and a little girl flying; she kept the drawing which is reproduced here. The sky in the background and the sea were executed with the air brush, using the procedures I explain on the previous page.

First stage: transferring the drawing, and painting with the air brush (Fig. 423)
After the study of the girl and sea-gulls is traced onto the fine watercolor paper with a hard well-sharpened pencil, Maria frames the illustration with scotch tape previously discharged of its glue, by means of rubbing it on the edge of the table. Next, she paints the sky and sea with the air brush. She first applies a blue-green background creating the sky and nearly obliterating the pencil drawn figures. Using the same color, Maria Rius paints a series of five undulating stripes through a templet or stencil, applying paint as she moves the templet down. Thus, beginning at the top, the second stripe is darker still, and so on. "In

the fourth stripe," I told Maria, "the templet has dirtied the edge." "Have you noticed?" she replied in an amusing way, "I've seen it; it wasn't planned. It's a shame, but I thought that I could paint the foam and win in the end."

Second stage: painting the foreground and drawing the figures (Fig. 424)

Maria Rius carefully removes the transparent scotch tape covering the lower part of the illustration, and paints this area, working with a no. 8 brush and a light, yellow green color, to represent the beach. Below this color, as a decorative border for the illustration, she now paints some green shapes that remind us of trees and bushes. The interesting point here is that in order to paint the beach and bushes, Maria Rius has had to wash this area which was previously painted with green color from the air brush. She must also dilute and wash off the paint which covers the flying girl and sea-gulls. This is one of the tricks the watercolor illustrator knows. This is a job that the illustrator will do quite often. The artist will rely on the more malleable quality of liquid watercolors to help her. She first wets the shapes with the brush and then absorbs the diluted paint with a paper towel, repeating the procedure—always using clean water—as many times as is necessary to leave the treated areas free of color. This is obviously harder to do if the color is very intense or if the pigment is very permanent, as in the case of carmine, alizarin crimson, Prussian blue; emerald, and several others.

Beside this procedure, the artist may also rely on a trick, which consists of washing the whitened zone with lye diluted in water—this leaves the paper absolutely white! (Beware: while applying the diluted lye do *not* use a brush with marten hair, but a brush with synthetic hair, the only material that will resist the corrosive action of lye.)

Third stage: painting the figure (Fig. 425)

Once you know the system of washing and the trick with lye, it's no secret how the sea foam was "painted," or how the sea-gulls acquired their whiteness. But there is something left that deserves a separate discussion.

Maria has removed the remaining scotch tape creating a bright, clean rectangle around the illustration, and has begun painting the flying girl. She paints the color of the flesh first, next the rose color of the dress, and finally the reddish Sienna hair. In each case, especially in

424

425

Fig. 424—Good illustrations are actually the products of patient and delicate work. Here, for example Maria Rius has had to absorb the color of the the air brush at the bottom of the illustration, to paint the beach and bushes in the foreground. She has "opened up" white areas for the seagulls and girl, but not satisfied with the absorption effected by hand with the brush and blotting paper, she has patiently applied liquid bleach diluted with water to achieve the results she is after.

fig. 425—Here Maria Rius is "opening up" the blanks shown in the previous figure; a job which requires maximum precision so as not to "go too far,"

painting an illustration in watercolors

Fig. 426—Here is a curious anecdote in connection with this picture. Maria Rius had not planned to paint the white foam on the peaks of the waves. Something unexpected happened: on finishing the last of these blends, Maria forgot to dry the edge of the stencil, and when she lifted it, seeing these small stains as dots on the crest of the second wave (see them in fig. 424), she was desperate. "The whole job wasted," she exclaimed aloud. But at that moment she found a solution and said smiling, happily, "Good, I shall paint the foam of the sea waves. I remember the master Corot, who said that when painting there is always, in addition, 'the happy accident' which sometimes brings about a change, an idea which enriches the painting."

426

the skin and dress, Maria uses the same technique she will later apply to the sea-gulls, and earlier used to create the bushes and trees at the bottom of the painting. This is how it works: Maria applies a layer of watercolor. Almost immediately after she partially removes the color by blotting the area with absorbent paper. She applies a new coat and blots again, over and over, until she gets the desired intensity. At the same time she is modeling the figure, shaping the form with contrasts of light and shadow. This procedure reminds me of the method employed by the old masters of oil painting, the Flemish and Renaissance artists, who painted with fine transparent glazes, one layer on top of another, achieving a transparent, even finish.

Figs. 427, 428—The final stage in illustration is finishing up, adjusting, profiling, touching up, completing. The technique of Maria Rius, and of many contemporary illustrators, involves applying liquid watercolor glazes, using colored pencils (Caran D'Ache brand) to shape volume and heighten color and using a hard 4H grading pencil to accentuate forms, graying and toning down areas with extremely fine twirls invisible to the naked eye.

427

Fourth stage: the finishing touches (Figs. 427 and 428)

In this figure and the next, we view the last stage, realized with a procedure that is truly unique: the intermingling of three mediums—watercolor, lead pencil, and color pencils. With these tools the artist models the forms, and strengthens contours. Both the lead pencil —4H, which happens to be a very hard pencil —and the color pencils, will create subtle gray ues, applied in minuscule strokes, dots, hardly noticeable at first glance, but which will give the illustration a warm finely pebbled texture when it is reduced for reproduction in a book. With the lead pencil and color pencils, Maria Rius models and completes the hair. She draws the features of the face, she models the delicate folds of the dress, the girl's hands and feet, and gives volume to the swallows... All a difficult task, requiring technique, craftsmanship, and creativity.

painting an illustration in watercolors

painting a snowy landscape in watercolors

I painted this same subject in watercolor in January of this year, and I will now paint it again, but this time in the studio, and explain the process in detail, not just showing the various stages of development in the painting of the work, but also the different processes and techniques.

This is the last of the step-by-step demonstrations presented in this book: a painting designed to be a final project, which I will paint for you myself, using many of the concepts, theories, and techniques that a professional uses when painting. I hope that this will be a complete lesson, summarizing the things I have tried to teach you in the pages of this book.

To start with, look at figs. 429 and 430 which show the painting I did on the scene and a photo of the subject, and notice how useful it is to take the camera along when you go out to paint. With a photograph of the subject, you can compare the finished painting to the real image, and even rectify or finish some details later on, when the original scene in life is quite changed. Now then, starting with the photo and the painting I did, notice first that the scene offers a compositional scheme which I tried to accent, as you can see in the adjoining figures. Notice the differences between the painting and the actual scene; these are changes I made during the process of interpreting: (1) suppressing those long trees beside the fence that surrounds the town, on the left-hand side, because they interfere with a view of the town; (2) interpreting the roofs as covered with snow, even though they actually were not; (3) suppressing three of the trees which appear in the ditch running diagonally across the landscape, and distributing them differently so that they will not interfere with our view of the town; (4) changing the diagonal ditch into a slight ridge, which lends variety to the composition, and allows the addition of the blue band of shadow thrown by the ridge, which aids the composition; (5) heightening the shadows of the trees on the ridge, adding variety to the scene; and (6) reducing the height of the gray band of the village and darkening the ochre color in the railing in the foreground, in order to better emphasize the geometric zig-zag form which determines the composition of the painting.

Now let us look at the resolution of this water-

430

Fig. 429—(Top) Photograph of the snow-covered landscape which will be used as a subject for the watercolor of this last demonstration. The landscape of the photograph corresponds to this scheme of composition.

Fig. 430—(Left) A watercolor painting made a year ago, of the landscape shown in the previous photograph (429). The interpretation of the subject using this scheme heightens the geometrical shape and improves the composition of the painting.

color painting, step by step. But first, allow me a brief commentary on the materials and tools used, and on my work habits.

When I paint outdoors, whether in the city or the country, I paint with a typical tripod of the box-case-tripod type. I have no objection to artists who paint with their paper almost vertical—a tablet or mounted on a board, as many artists do—but I am more comfortable with the tablet or board tilted at an angle of 35 or 40 degrees, as are many other artists. This preference means that in the studio, I always work with a tabletop easel in the form of a lectern, and an adjustable seat wich can be raised somewhat higher than normal. I connect the table or sheet of paper with clips;

painting a snowy landscape in watercolors

that way I never have to wet and dry the paper with it already mounted with tape (see fig. 431). I find it more practical to paint with the paper on the tablet, or with a sheet of paper thick enough that it can be adequately mounted with clips. I use tube paints and damp tablets of paint interchangeably. While paint recently squeezed from a tube facilitates rapid execution—you don't have to rub with a brush to pick up the color—by the time it has been on the palette for two or three days, it has just about the same texture as damp tablets do. So in the long run, both types are fine. I use pads of paper made by Fabriano, or Arches or Canson, of medium or coarse grain, and brushes of sable hair in nos. 6, 8, 12, and 14, and occasionally a no. 18 ox-hair brush and a Japanese stag-hair brush with flat bristles, the latter two for washes, and wide gray areas, as well as for dampening large areas with water. I also use a natural sponge for dampening, for example, before beginning a painting—and also, on occasion, to wash, wipe, reduce, draw, and lighten. I use H pencils, which smear the least, and an ordinary white plastic eraser (I don't like kneaded erasers, which feel like modeling clay).

I use only one container of water, which I change every once in a great while—since I kind of like dirty water for painting. When I paint in the studio, I put the container of water on top of a cloth rag, folded into four layers. This protects the table from water, and also serves as a means of removing water or paint from the brush. All I do is "paint" the rag with the brush a little bit before I touch the paper. And as regards to emptying the brush, I have waited until the end to mention the use of absorbent paper of the paper towel type sold in rolls for kitchen use. As you know, these towels are made of a spongy paper, which dries rapidly and easily absorbs the water and dampness of the watercolors. I use them constantly, having a folded or crumpled towel al-

432

Fig. 431—Painting in watercolors, whether in the open air or in the studio, I feel better working with the board inclined at an angle of some 30° to 45°. In the studio this requires a tabletop easel in the form of a lectern (fig. 98) and an adjustable seat which can be raised somewhat higher than normal.

Fig. 432—A detail of no importance but which I believe is useful: under the water bottle I place a piece of absorbent cloth, folded several times, which apart from protecting the table against drops and wetness, enables me to remove excess water from the brush by simply pressing, as if I were painting on the cloth.

ways available in my left hand, to clean the brush, reduce, absorb, blend or break down color, pressing, more or less, on a recently painted area. Sometimes I even use it to draw, as sometimas happens with a uniform background of sky, when simply pressing with the paper towel can "open up" a white spot which, if properly treated afterwards, can become a magnificent bank of cumulus clouds. And now let us return to the watercolor painting of a snowy landscape.

First stage: drawing and reserving whites (Fig. 434)

We begin, as always, with a precise, well defined line drawing, particularly in the area of the village houses, where the buildings and roofs must correspond to reality; the same is true of the ditch in the middleground and the trees appearing there. But the trunks and delicate branches of the trees in the foreground may, on the other hand, be drawn with more liberty, representing, for the time being, the largest trunks.

Afterwards, I apply masking fluid with a no. 4 synthetic brush, covering the areas where I wish to preserve the white, these being: the roofs of the houses and the walls which surround the village, the small snowy areas of the mountains and their upper profiles, and the broadest trunks of the slender trees in the foreground. I also paint a little fluid in the right foreground to create some snowdrifts. It is very important to use masking fluid in the right quantity and not to overdo it; avoid reserving whites when normal watercolor techniques can be used.

Next I reserve a patch of white—using white wax—in the thin promontory on the left side of the village (indicated as A in the figure adjoining this first stage) and in the band of terrain in the center (B). In zone A, I reinforce this reserve of white created with white wax by applying masking fluid, scrubbing and graduating it from the top down (as you know, masking fluid is cream or light blue in color, which makes it easy to locate later on).

Second stage: painting the sky, the mountains, and the village houses (Fig. 440)

Before beginning to paint, let me mention that

Fig. 433—Working, painting with the brush in the right hand; under the left hand is a piece of blotting paper folded twice or more, always ready to allow you to remove any excess paint from the brush, to blot the color in a specific area, and to "draw" by opening up white areas in a form or a color which has been applied. The tissue paper or blotting paper, which mops up like paper towels used in the kitchen, is essential for watercolor painting.

433

434

Fig. 434—Here is the finished drawing, with the masking fluid applied to reserve certain areas, visible by its bluish color.

Fig. 435—Application of masking fluid to reserve certain areas with a synthetic no. 4 brush. The fluid which remains on the brush is diluted with water to wash it before it has dried; but some fluid always remains which has to be eliminated by squeezing the brush and pulling it through your fingers and nails.

435

painting a snowy landscape in watercolors

the scale of broken colors, and their cold feeling in this watercolor, are the product of a mixture of dark sepia and ultramarine blue, which gives a basic neutral gray that can be altered (as it has been) by mixing with carmine, ochre, emerald green, and Prussian blue, in order to obtain the different colors and nuances visible in my interpretation of the scene. For example, the sky was painted with the two basic colors mentioned above—ultramarine blue and dark sepia—by adding carmine a little bit a time, using a lot of water, of course.

I customarily test color mixtures on a separate piece of paper, or in the margins of the painting itself, as you will see I am doing in fig. 436.

I begin painting the sky with the color mentioned above, applying it to the group of houses, the mountains, and the sky itself, painting with the tablet of paper turned upside down (fig. 437) in order to achieve a wash that builds up color in the higher part of the sky and leaves the horizon slightly lighter. While the wash is still damp, I "draw" some white clouds with a paper towel by pressing on the area of the horizon and removing color. Without waiting for the sky wash to dry completely, I rapidly paint the mountains with a darker gray-blue wash, consistent in color but softened and diffused at the edges with a clean brush. This wash extends to the group of houses and to the village. On the edge of the house at the left hand side of the village, I "open up" a light spot like a cloud of smoke, using a small stick with a cotton swab on the end (of course, the cotton absorbs the water, and with it, the color: fig. 439). Now I must wait until the second wash—for the mountains and houses —dries I speed up the drying by using a hair dryer, and then begin painting the houses,

436

437

438

Fig. 436—I select from the samples of colors in the white enameled palette, but before actually painting it I check the color on a separate paper or in the margin of the paper on which I am going to paint the watercolor, as you can see in this picture.

Fig. 437—To paint an even colored sky, one trick is to turn the board upside down.

439

Fig. 439—Now with a small stick with a swab of cotton on the end, I absorb color and open up bright areas like clouds of smoke on the top edge of the houses.

Fig. 438—When the gray of the sky has still not completely dried, I paint the darker gray of the hills with which I also cover the forms of the houses and the town.

fences, and yards of the village, with different nuances and with similar but diverse colors. I continue to use dark sepia mixed with ultramarine blue as the base, varying the amounts and proportions to obtain grays which are either bluer, darker, or more neutral, without forgetting the possibility— the necessity—of bringing into play the ochre, carmine, Prussian and cobalt blue tones. I paint the doors and windows of the houses without outlining, without too much fuss, and call this second stage over.

In a watercolor such as this one—but actually in all watercolors—which uses a scale of colors with a notable blue-gray tendency, the artist must always feel the need to enrich the colors, painting with different paints and different nuances, trying to attain a tonal unity *within the* variety *of colors and nuances.*

Third stage: resolving the uneven ridge in the center (Fig. 441)

First I paint the trees, starting with the trunks, using dark Sienna and a little blue, finishing the fan-like branches afterward with a no. 6 sable brush and controlling the intensity with light, absorbent touches of the paper towel. Next, I turn my attention to the shadows in the gulley and the gray-blue shadow on the ridge or uneven land next to the gulley, where the long shadows of the trees also appear. I made this gray-blue color by first mixing a base of Sienna and ultramarine blue, and then adding cobalt blue and a pinch of carmine. I will paint the upper edges of these bands with the *frottis* or dry brush technique.

The *frottis* or dry brush technique—also called "scumbling"—(fig. 245-247) demands constant tests, carried out on separate paper of the same quality and grain as the paper being used for the painting. Naturally this technique cannot be used on recently painted, damp surfaces.

I paint with this technique in the areas mentioned above (testing it on a separate piece of paper first, in order to know how much to dampen or dry the brush), controlling the dry brushstrokes with light and precise dabs of the paper towel, pressing and absorbing color, blending more or less, etc. Then I use the blue-gray mixture to paint the shadows of the trees and the graduation of this same color which appears on the right hand side, as well as the shadow of the ridge, always using the dry brush technique (fig. 441).

440

Fig. 440—In this second stage it is possible to see the need to diversify the color, particularly on the fronts and roofs of the houses, on the land, and on the fences. This diversity, which is always a good idea, is particularly necessary when, as in this case, the subject suggests a marked gray tendency.

painting a snowy landscape in watercolors

Fig. 441—It is important to paint *straight off*, without stressing anything, trying to achieve success with the first application and brushing without fear. This also involves the technique known as scumbling or dry brush, which makes it possible to blend with miniscule dots or spots caused by the rubbing of the half-dry brush on the grain of the paper. The success of this technique depends largely on trying the effect out on a separate piece of paper first, and on working carefully with the blotting paper to eliminate or remove color if necesarry.

441

Fourth stage: finishing the gulley and resolving the foreground (Fig. 447)

To finish off the middleground of the gulley, I paint in the interior with grays, Siennas, and blues corresponding to the rocks and clods of earth not covered with snow, the bushes and clumps of grass, etc. This is a laborious task calling for a fine brush, but there is still room for interpretation and sythesis. But, hey! Wait a minute! The crest of the ridge, at the edge of the blue band, seems poorly explained and narrow. It would be better if I could extend it, and I will, using the sandpaper technique.

First I wrap the eraser end of a pencil with a piece of sandpaper, then I energetically rub the area just above and beyond the limit of the area mentioned above, in a movement parallel to that area. This "opens" and widens the white area. Afterward I clean the area with my eraser (fig. 442, 443). Then I touch up this new, "open" area and blend it in.

I begin now to paint the wall of the lower right-hand side, as well as the snow on the land in the left foreground, resolving them with the dry brush technique. Attention should be paid to the direction of the brushstrokes here, which should be diagonal for the snow, descending from left to right, parallel to the diagonal of the gulley and ridge. For the stones of the wall, which is free of snow, the brush-strokes should also be diagonal, but in the opposite direction, descending from right to left (see the diagram which accompanies fig. for a better understanding). These are the wide "frottis" sections, done with a wide brush, continuous and decided, and their success depends as much on the amount of paint and relative dampness of the brush,—which I will, of course, test beforehand many times—as on the simultaneous control exercised by the absorbent paper towel. I will begin with the snow on the left-hand side, using three color nuances: first, a neutral light gray, which serves as a base, breaking down and becoming lighter in color as it grows more distant from the foreground. As I have already mentioned, the *frottis* must be carried out with a broad brush and in a continuous and decided manner, therefore, I have taken the precaution of covering the edge of the wall with a piece of cardboard, as you can see in fig. 446. In this way, I avoid the risk of "running over the line," that is, running into the ochre of the wall at the end of those large, rapid strokes of the dry brush. Finally, to finish this fourth stage, I paint the snow in the foreground of the wall applying two coats of two different grays, the first, a light gray wich serves as a foundation, the second, alternating with the dry brush technique, drawing the forms the snow takes on in this area. As you can see, I also use small touches of siennas and blues to clarify these forms (fig. 447).

Fifth stage: peeling off the masking fluid and general touchup (Fig. 448)

Energetically rubbing with an ordinary every-day eraser, I remove the masking fluid from the mountains, the roofs of the houses, the mound and walls that surround the town and the trees and trunks in the foreground, leaving the snowdrifts for last.

Horrible, right? I want you to see this view, this moment (fig. 448), so that you can better understand the disagreeable surprise of these whites—so terribly white— that stand out by virtue of their excessive contrast, and that may lead us to believe that our trick with the masking fluid was a mistake. You will see that it is a good trick in the following stages, but obviously it should be used with caution. Now I begin to retouch, to blend these whites

442 **443**

Figs. 442, 443—"Opening up" a white with sandpaper, wound around the end of a pencil, and rubbing fairly energetically. When the rubbing is completed, the area must be cleaned with a rubber eraser, then touched up as necessary.

444

Fig. 444—Here is an enlarged picture of the snow and the wall in the foreground, which I am resolving with the "scumble" to more closely represent the texture of snow-covered surfaces.

445

Fig. 445—As you can see in this scheme, the direction of the brush differs depending on the place and the subject or element which is being painted.

446

Fig. 446—To paint here with the "scumble" (dry brush) technique and with these broad and long brush strokes and avoid "going too far," I have covered the wall on the right-hand side with a piece of card-board.

painting a snowy landscape in watercolors

Fig. 447—The white at the peak of the fringe or margin in the center is now broader, after having been widened by rubbing with sandpaper; the irregularities and dark shapes of the fringe have already been reviewed and reconstructed; in the foreground I have resolved the texture of the snow by using the "scumble" or dry brush technique: everything is ready for the removal of the masking fluid.

447

into the rest of the nuances and colors, graying them, dirtying and diffusing them patiently working with the point of a damp brush where their edges are too hard, painting the "holes" in the trees with blue-gray to represent the snow in the shade... and leaving it like that, as you can see in fig. 449.

Sixth stage: slender trees, snowdrifts and overall finishing (Fig. 450)

With a neutral black, made from dark Sienna and a little blue, I paint, or perhaps I should say draw, the profiles of the slender trees in the foreground, retaining the white strokes made by the masking fluid. For this I take advantage of the fine point of the no. 6 sable brush, with which I also trace the fine branches —so fine that I wind up drawing some of

Fig. 448—This is the state of the watercolor, once the masking fluid which reserved these blank areas has been removed. A result which is somewhat unpleasant, due to the excessive contrast and the lack of balance caused by these white areas against the color harmony of the watercolor in general, I hope that having seen this result, you will be aware of the fact that masking fluid to reserve certain areas is a good auxiliary for certain cases (to represent the flakes of snow, as we shall see further on, for example); but this technique should not be abused despite the good final result which I expect to achieve once these blanks have been harmonized.

448

them with a black ballopint pen. Afterward, I paint the few dry leaves with ochre, a little carmine, and a pinch of blue. Then I remove the masking fluid from the snow drifls and begin the final work of finish. With the black ballpoint pen I draw some almost imperceptible contours, in the fan-shaped drifts in the trees of the gulley, as well as some small branches. I outline the edges of some of the roofs and windows of the village houses.

Now I decide to open up some lighter, spherical-shaped areas on the left side of the village. I use the technique of opening whites with a synthetic brush, keeping in mind that these light areas correspond to hearty village trees which animate and diversify the forms. I continue with the sharp point of a blade or mat knife, "opening up" very fine points and lines,

painting a snowy landscape in watercolors

Fig. 449—The excesses have been smoothed and harmonized with light glazes which cover the "holes" which the masking fluid revealed. Just a few more touches to finish the painting.

Fig. 450—I paint the slim trees in the foreground with spontaneous, carefree strokes, using the dark liquid paint in such a way that the brush flows freely. There is no chance that with such a fine stroke I will end up with an excessively linear or too technical resolution. I give a few touches with a black ballpoint pen to the trees, the houses; I paint the eaves and remove the masking fluid over the snowflakes. I feel the cold air, the feeling of snow in the high mountain, and I am happy. I have finished.

449

scraping and scratching the paper in the snow-drifts, in the trees, on the branches of the slender trunks in the foreground, adding snow effects... always correcting—just little things, almost nothing—the color of a house, the color of the village wall, the color of the mound of earth...

Then I leave it alone, and sign it.

And now, I bid you adieu with the sincere wish that today, tomorrow, right now—partially by having read and looked at this book —you will feel the preeminent need to begin to paint a watercolor.